PRAISE FOR *UNLEASH YOUR IMAGINATION*

"*Unleash Your Imagination* encourages the reader to investigate deeply held values and beliefs and to view the future with an open mind and optimistic spirit."

—Thomas Moore, Ph.D., #1 *New York Times* bestselling author of *Care of the Soul,* available in a twenty-fifth anniversary edition.

"*Unleash Your Imagination* is a powerful affirmation of how each of us can apply design thinking to create a great life – not only to benefit ourselves but to be better for each other, too. Leveraging an optimism that we all have within, Dennis Kleidon provides resources to guide the decisions we can make as we choose with intention to be more creative, more engaged, and more fulfilled in and by our lives."

—Stuart I. Graff, President & CEO, Frank Lloyd Wright Foundation

"Daydreaming, imagining, visualizing are all abilities we have instinctively, and that make us human beings. When we allow ourselves to truly let our imaginations go and develop goals we want to accomplish – now or in the future – we are halfway there. Dennis Kleidon's *Unleash Your Imagination* provides us with the tools to help sharpen our creative imagining to bring our goals(s) to fruition and nourish that sometimes elusive right side of our brain. *All* of us will benefit from this encouraging book that provides clarity and sound guidance in the 'how to' of letting our creative spirits soar and become creative problem solvers in the process. This is a must read – especially for parents and teachers of our children."

—Barbara Rosen, Ph.D., Retired Clinical Psychologist, Vancouver

Unleash
Your
Imagination

Unleash Your Imagination

TRANSFORM YOUR LIFE

Dennis Kleidon

RIVER GROVE
BOOKS

Published by River Grove Books
Austin, Texas
www.rivergrovebooks.com

Distributed by River Grove Books

Cover image: cropped from Transformation #2, a painting by Dennis Kleidon in acrylic on canvas. For information about the author, his paintings, or public speaking, visit www.denniskleidon.com.

Publisher's Cataloging-in-Publication data is available.

Print ISBN: 978-1-63299-568-1

eBook ISBN: 978-1-63299-569-8

First Edition

THIS BOOK IS DEDICATED TO MY WIFE, ROSE

Rose has always been an inspiration and has encouraged all my creative endeavors. She has graciously offered advice and guidance during the writing of *Unleash Your Imagination* and provided expertise as the editor of this book. To her I offer my sincere appreciation for her knowledge and wisdom and for her dedication to making this book a reality.

APPRECIATION

As I formed concepts and ideas for this book, I had the privilege of reading and meeting with many authors who influenced me and reinforced the thoughts and ideas of the book. An important purpose of this book is to gather a broad range of comments from others about the ideas of positivity, optimism, and the uses of imagination, and for that reason, and to honor them and bring attention to their beliefs, I included quotations from many of these authors. Their dedication to excellence inspired me to expand my work as a designer, artist, and writer and to continue pursuing my creative research.

I and my editorial team have striven in every instance of quoting and attributing to abide by fair use principles, as this book has an educational purpose. I appreciate being able to include the wisdom of these authors in my book and have made every attempt to represent them accurately. There is much to learn and understand about the many approaches to living an exceptional life. Studying these authors can be a strong foundation for your pursuit of personal excellence.

The reading list in Appendix C is a bibliography which I encourage you to use as a guide for further study. The books on it are filled with wonderful concepts that will help you make decisions on your pathway to a well-designed life of excellence.

INSPIRATIONS

"You never finish designing your life – life is a joyous and never-ending design project of building your way forward."

—Bill Burnett

"No matter how great your teachers ... [and] how esteemed your academy ..., eventually you will have to do the work by yourself. Eventually, the teachers won't be there anymore...and you'll be on your own. The hours that you will then put into practice, study, auditions, and creation will be entirely up to you. The sooner and more passionately you get married to this idea – that it is ultimately entirely up to you – the better off you'll be."

—Elizabeth Gilbert

"Life is not about longevity as much as it is about intensity. If you have many, many years of tepid living, of what value is that? But if you have a few years of vitality and conviviality, you may feel that you have really lived. Life is not a quantity but a quality."

—Thomas Moore

"You never change things by fighting the existing reality. To change something, build a new model that makes the existing model obsolete."

—Buckminster Fuller

"Everything can be taken from a man but one thing: the last of the human freedoms—to choose one's attitude in any given set of circumstances, to choose one's own way."

—Victor Frankl

"The longer I live, the more beautiful life becomes. If you foolishly ignore beauty, you will soon find yourself without it. But if you invest in beauty, it will remain with you all the days of your life."

—Frank Lloyd Wright

"You elevate your life by taking responsibility for who you are and what you're choosing to become. You can transcend the ordinary, mundane, and average with thoughts of greater joy and meaning; you can decide to elevate your life, rather than have it stagnate or deteriorate with excuses. Go beyond where you presently are."

—Wayne Dyer

"Curiosity about life in all its aspects…is the secret of great creative people."

—Leo Burnett

"A master in the art of living draws no sharp distinction between his work and his play; his labor and his leisure; his mind and his body; his education and his recreation. He hardly knows which is which. He simply pursues his vision of excellence through whatever he is doing, and leaves others to determine whether he is working or playing. To himself, he always appears to be doing both."

—Danielle LaPorte

"Whether or not you are aware of it, deep in your heart there is something you've always wanted to accomplish. Not just a fleeting wish but a deep intention that may have begun to grow in your heart while you were still very young. This is your dearest dream, your ultimate concern. When you identify and nurture your deepest desire, it can become a source of great happiness, energy, and motivation. It can provide you with drive, with direction."

—Thich Nhat Hanh

CONTENTS

PREFACE

Because you selected this book, I know a lot about you.

1. YOU CARE. You are concerned about your life and the lives of your family and friends.
2. YOU WANT TO CHANGE. You have a deep desire to improve your existing reality, are dedicated to self-improvement and to making needed changes.
3. YOU WANT BIG CHANGES. You want to create a life that is exceptional and that uses all your talents and abilities.
4. YOU WANT THOUGHTFUL CHANGES. You care about the quality of your life and wish to live your everyday life by your values, principles, and beliefs.
5. YOU WANT TO REALIZE YOUR FULL POTENTIAL. As you learn more about how to do this, it will empower you and help you help others to realize their potential as well.
6. YOU CARE ABOUT OTHERS. You want to contribute to society, and as your life progresses, you want to leave a legacy for those who listen to you now and who will come after you well into the future.

Have I come close to knowing you? I hope so. These are the reasons you picked up this book, were intrigued by the title and are searching for another way – a way to unlock your dreams and aspirations in search of a life of excellence. I have taught thousands of college students over my lifetime and have worked with hundreds of CEOs in a variety of businesses and have seen the same curiosity about life and self-improvement in their actions and in their pursuit of self-investigation and learning.

This book shows how to use design thinking to challenge your normal routines, allow your imagination to run wild, and harness that imagination to shape a direction guided by your life's purpose. I have been trained as an architectural and graphic designer, have taught and practiced the design process throughout my career. I approach change and creativity from a designer's point of view, using a problem-solving and creative development process. This is both analytical and creative, replacing blank-page panic with the thrill of new possibilities. If used with an open mind and curious spirit, the designer's approach leads to many fresh solutions you may never have considered.

I wrote this book to help you open your mind and discover new opportunities for your life. I want to help you think through the process of change by using your imagination to unleash your long-standing desires and find a way to integrate them into your current life by making easy, gradual, changes to your daily patterns. These changes can lead the way to an enhancement of the quality of your life and to go beyond yourself to contribute to the world.

As I began thinking about this book, I created a list of intriguing words and ideas. To do a deep evaluation of our life and develop exciting plans, we need to stretch our imagination and use all the creative potential within us to imagine exciting solutions. I began by choosing concepts vital for self-evaluation and exploring how each might influence our personal research, discovery, and decision-making.

KEY WORDS AND IDEAS

Optimism	Fantasizing	Creativity
Pretending	Experimentation	Contemplation
Innovation	Enthusiasm	Harmony
Expectation	Feelings	Visualization
Wishes	Idealization	Open-Mindedness

Motivation	Imagination	Dreams
Obsessions	Inspiration	Hope
Invention	Passion	Joy
Transformation	Aspiration	Excitement
Perspective	Curiosity	Desires
Brainstorming	Anticipation	Positive Thinking
Perception	Enlightenment	Confidence
Meaning	Happiness	Purpose

These words and concepts are guides to this book. As I wrote, I was intrigued by the multitude of connections such ideas made with each other. Together, they influence our creative investigation, and if integrated into planning, can lead to exciting discoveries and experiences that stretch our imagination.

It's a new day. We don't have to live it the way we always have or stay the way we are today. We can improve, change and make dramatic shifts in our life, changes we have been wanting for decades. Besides that, the journey itself is exciting. It's an expedition filled with surprise, discovery, and new adventure.

Does this sound scary? Perhaps. But just think for a minute. You have only one life: this one, the one you are living right now. It has begun, and it will end. The question is, what are you going to do with this life between now and the end? At whatever age, you need to give serious attention to the conditions of your current reality and see how you can imagine and then create an extraordinary life for yourself.

Today, almost all of us have more freedom than human beings have ever had. Tens of thousands of years ago, we freed ourselves from the food chain, and every advance since that has increased our freedom. Today, most of us are free from hunger, from heat, cold and exposure, from ignorance and superstition. We are even free to enjoy a "second childhood" in the best sense, a "retirement" when little is required of us and we are free to enjoy life our way.

So why not create a vision for an extraordinary future and fill this future with new adventures, exciting places, and fantastic relationships? Why not? You own your life. Design it to your specs. Build it any way you want. Once this life is over, that's it. So, make this one the best, every day, every week, every year until your last breath.

As you will see as you read *Unleash Your Imagination,* we don't become innovative by following the leader. We need to break loose, un-focus and deal with life's decisions with a more innovative spirit. Our subconscious mind is filled with ideas just waiting to be discovered.

It may be scary, but it's also exciting: a life that we imagine, we create, we design, and for which we develop a new vision. A perfect vision. Everything in place just the way we want it. Does this sound impossible? It might, depending on your current reality. But I know that this approach to change will allow you to open your mind, unleash your imagination and create a life you have only dreamed of. It will bring you into a new phase of your life with a fresh and optimistic spirit and a level of excitement you may not have experienced before.

One of the things influencing this book is that for more than three decades I raced sailboats and participated in regattas. Those of you who are sailors know that at the beginning of a race, you chart a course to get to your destination. However, during your voyage on the water, the winds change, a bigger ship arrives unexpectedly and gets in the way of your charted course, the winds die, and you drift for a while, or the tides change, and you must go with the flow – literally. However, you still know where you want to go. You have charted your course and destination, and you make adjustments along the way to counteract the obstacles and eventually get to your destination.

This book looks at the processes involved in designing your life with creativity and imagination. Life is not just analytical. Your dreams and desires need to surface for you to enjoy true happiness and excitement. Through creative thinking and the stimulation of your imagination, you can make decisions that expose your subconscious dreams and desires.

These decisions will allow you to approach life planning with imagination and innovation to achieve a happier and more exciting life.

I have had an extraordinary life working as a university professor, owner of a marketing communications firm and a publishing company. I have developed and launched products internationally and have worked with my staff to create and implement targeted marketing campaigns. In the classroom, I have worked with thousands of students who opened their minds, unleashed their imagination and experimented with the processes of designing and problem-solving. I have had the privilege of working with CEOs from large and small businesses and have learned an enormous amount from these experiences. I have worked with hundreds of business owners who hired our marketing communications firm to provide creative and imaginative solutions for marketing their products or services. And I have seen CEOs succeed and fail in their attempts to grow their companies. Throughout this book, I will share many of the ideas I learned from these experiences.

Thank you again for your desire to improve your life and for entrusting me to guide you through the process of discovery. Open your mind, be curious and enjoy the journey. Let me offer my congratulations and thank you for embarking upon a journey of change. You are not doing this just for yourself, because when you live a richer, more well-resolved life, the riches of your life enrich us all.

Only when we choose to believe that we live in a world where challenges can be overcome, our behavior matters, and change is possible, can we summon all our drive, energy, and emotional and intellectual resources to make that change happen.

—Shawn Achor

INTRODUCTION

HOW TO LIVE AN EXTRAORDINARY LIFE

We are defined by the narrative that we write for ourselves every day. Is it a story of joy, perseverance, love, and kindness, or is it a story of guilt, blame, bitterness, and failure? Find a new vocabulary to match the emotions and feelings that you want to live by. Talk to yourself with love.

—Jay Shetty

What keeps you from living an extraordinary life? What is holding you back from making decisions that will help you realize your dreams? Sometimes the whole process seems simple:

1. DESIRE. Develop a burning desire to have or do something.
2. PLAN. Make a plan that will allow you to accomplish your desired goal.
3. ACT. Just go out and do it.

If only it were that simple. Each of us is influenced by our past, our friends, our family, our job, our religion, our education, and all sorts of other things that set the patterns for our life. Each of us has responsibilities, physical and emotional limitations, schedules, and budgets. These influences can be positive for establishing a stable life, but they can also inhibit our imagination and be barriers to achieving our dreams.

Besides that, and perhaps even more crippling, excuses surround us! Time, people and commitments provide excellent excuses for not making decisions and for deferring actions that could help us accomplish important things. But, by unleashing your imagination and allowing your dreams and wishes to surface, you can harness a powerful new force, using newfound creativity and design thinking to work around whatever gets in your way, reach your goals, and achieve your preferred future.

We have been trained to approach decision-making with rational, logical thinking. That's fine as far as it goes, but unfortunately, an analytical approach can de-power the imagination and hobble our ability to see innovative solutions. Creative thinking is vital to re-inventing life and planning a spectacular future. If we are to be inventive in our businesses and personal life, we need to change the way we think and discard routines that stifle our imaginative potential.

Approaching life with an open mind and a spirit of curiosity will inspire more innovative solutions in your search for answers.

Creativity uses the right side of the brain, and exercising this side can lead to the transformational power of getting in touch with your own creativity. Unleashing your imagination helps you tap into reservoirs of innovation and revel in the joys of discovery. Perhaps, most importantly, it can be the source for a new vision of a more extraordinary life.

Life does not have to just happen to us. You can create it. You are the designer of your life, and you can make the choices that will decide your future and decisions that will affect your life. By opening your subconscious mind and unleashing your imagination, you can discover many more opportunities for creating an exceptional life filled with new opportunities and excitement.

Deciding to embrace optimism is the only choice if you wish to advance to a more extraordinary life. But you must make that decision. When you choose optimism, all of the options you have in life are more likely to succeed. This is what I would urge you to remember:

1. You are in control of your life.
2. You control your future.
3. You can decide to realize your full potential on a day-to-day basis and for a lifetime.
4. Your decisions can chart a course for a happier, more productive life.

These are bold statements, but the success of your life starts with decisions you make. And the more preparation you do to support your decisions, the more successful the results will be.

All kinds of influences could shape the decisions you make in your personal and business life. But you can govern those influences and balance them with a clearly written plan for the future – a plan guided by your wishes and dreams. If you allow outside influences to control your daily decisions and the long-term direction of your lives, they will not only influence today's activities, but establish a direction for your entire life.

It is up to each of us to chart the course for all aspects of our life, despite the influences of our business, our friends, our family, our spouse and people we meet every day. We are influenced by the education we received, our religious affiliations, the media and even our government. These influences can be positive or damaging. That is why we need to design a clear direction for our future that clarifies all aspects of our life.

The first decision to make is whether to proceed through life with a positive or negative attitude. This seems to be a ridiculously easy question. Who would choose to be negative? But do you know people who have a negative attitude about nearly everything they do? Has that worked for them? Do you enjoy being with them? Not likely. On the other hand, do you know people who are almost always upbeat and have a positive approach to life? These are people we are drawn to, whose energized, effective life we naturally want to share.

Why would people choose a sad, negative approach to life? What possible benefit could there be in choosing to live this way? Perhaps they haven't thought about it. Or maybe they haven't taken control of their lives. Maybe they haven't even realized that they have the power to make decisions for their lives. Maybe they are Eeyores, who cling to perpetual pessimism, as unwarranted and damaging as it is. Danielle LaPorte says:

> Self-doubt is so insidious that it not only renders us stuck in our lives, but it also actually weakens our ability to dream about what living unleashed would look like. And here's the thing: The mere

act of dreaming is a vitalizing, life-affirming endeavor. As it turns out, using your imagination is very, very good for your well-being. Einstein believed that imagination was even more important than knowledge itself.

If you find negative thoughts intruding, resolve to break that habit and train yourself to see things more positively. You can learn to look at life with optimism. You can use the tools and attitudes in this book and many other books to plan a spectacular life for yourself. We all know life can be a tremendous challenge. It takes all our effort and intelligence to make it what we wish it to be. And it takes a spirit of imagination to unleash the most innovative solutions. With that spirit of imagination, we can achieve what would otherwise be only naïveté. We can begin to believe this instead:

LIFE IS A WONDERFUL EXPERIENCE.

I AM IN CONTROL OF MY DESTINY.

When you take control of your life, unleash your imagination, focus on your future, and refuse to complain, no matter how many obstacles life has thrown at you, you can rebuild your life. By using your imagination, you can find new approaches through creative discovery. When you use abstract thinking, you can uncover those dreams and desires hidden in your subconscious. Let them surface, and let them be a guide to your future. It's time to be positive about who you are and where you are going. As Simon Sinek says, "Being for something…is about feeling inspired. Being *for* ignites the human spirit and fills us with hope and optimism."

And yet, this book is not about happiness. There are so many books written about happiness that the whole concept can get confusing. Why are people seeking happiness when happiness is only a state of being? This book is a guide to building a more exciting life, one driven by purpose, one filled with enthusiasm and one that harnesses your dreams and ambitions and leads you to accomplishments that you never knew were possible.

If you have had significant success, you might be resting on your laurels, wasting time in a contented state, while opportunities pass you by. And yet we all have enormous potential, a responsibility to our society and an ability to contribute. It's about finding purpose and crafting a purpose-driven life. We can unleash our imagination and our dreams to envision a future for ourselves that expands our horizons and opens doors that have been closed for decades. We are significant, and we can have a tremendous impact on issues that need to be addressed in our society, our profession, and our lives.

If we have a powerful, clearly defined purpose, we can use it to guide an extraordinary life. *Unleash* can help you use your imagination to discover your passions and find your purpose. And it will help you clarify the key questions that can guide you toward an exciting future.

We don't need just happiness. We don't need only to be content. We need to take action, find out "why," surpass our own limitations, and exceed our expectations. We need to envision a new future, multiply our abilities, and envision a life that may only live in our imagination. Once we see it, we can achieve it. Our life can be extraordinary, one that we generate and one that surpasses our more modest goals. We can stretch our imagination to build a life guided by superior expectations and excellence. Through harnessing our talents and abilities, focusing our dreams and imagination, we can build a life of significance.

o n e

UNLEASH YOUR DREAMS

OPEN YOUR MIND

Keep your mind open to change at all times. Welcome it. Court it. It is only by examining and reexamining your opinions and ideas that you can progress.

—Dale Carnegie

THIS BOOK IS ALL ABOUT CHANGE. Change in your current life. Change in your thinking. Change in your future. And all of this is good. All of what I will be proposing in this book will help you make plans for a more exciting and more extraordinary life. That's what we all want—the best that we can be and experience in this wonderful life we have been given. Always keep in mind, I'm on your side. My goals are to guide you through some serious thinking about your life and to help you

- manifest what you want to accomplish in your life,
- understand the problems and roadblocks along the way, and
- develop a direction for a new life—one that fulfills your desires and dreams for the future.

As you read the various chapters in this book, try to approach your research and planning with an open mind. This is essential for your true dreams to emerge and for you to discover the most critical barriers to achieving your desires.

We are all influenced by our routines in life, the status quo, and the patterns we have selected for our daily schedule. But, to discover who we really are and to understand our values and principles, we need to approach our research with a mind that is open and accepting of new thinking. We are constantly bombarded with responsibilities, schedules, news, colleagues, and family who demand our time.

Clearing your plate and making time for yourself as you journey through this book may mean adjusting your schedule. You will want time to work on various exercises that will help you discover yourself and choose your desired future. It may mean reserving days for research or assigning an hour a day to reflect on your life, your ambitions, your aspirations, and your dreams. This is important, because it is your life you want to change for the better. Do not get stuck in the rut of someone else's schedule. Plan a daily schedule that is right for you, one that allows free time for research, thinking and planning. This is an exciting experience if you approach it with a positive attitude and optimism.

Do not let your past overly influence your future. The past is just that, the past. You are living now, not in the past, and you have your future expectations to generate a high level of excitement. Reducing the influence of the past is one way of opening your mind.

We are all influenced by past experiences, which can be good or bad. Each of these experiences plays a part in forming our personalities, attitudes, and beliefs. Unfortunately, these experiences also shape our perceptions of life and cause us to develop predilections in our thinking. We need to put these aside as we begin this journey of self-discovery. In *Getting Back to Happy*, Marc and Angel Chernoff suggest this about letting go of the past:

> Sooner or later, you will realize that it's not what you lose along the way that counts; it's what you do with what you still have. When you let go of the past, forgive what needs forgiving, and move forward, you in no way change the past—you change the present and the future.

I would like you to take out a pen and several pieces of paper and write out answers to the following lists.

INFRINGEMENTS

1. List all your responsibilities.
2. List all the problems that you are facing.
3. List all the people who are getting in your way of succeeding.
4. List all the things that you do not enjoy doing in your life.
5. List things that annoy you.
6. List the things that you want to stop doing.
7. List things that you fear.
8. List things that get in the way of your happiness.

Feel free to add to these lists as fits your personal situation. Once you have made out these lists, take a careful look and evaluate them. Are there any that sound petty now that you see them in black and white? Maybe you are already beyond a few of these or are ready to accept or eliminate some. See if you can make any connections. Can any of these be combined? Are some more important than others?

Now, step back, put the answers to these lists in an envelope and place it in the lowest drawer in your desk. Now forget about the lists and the answers. As you forget about each problem and each list, feel your mind becoming freer, more open, and less encumbered by the problems in your past. The problems have been set aside. You are now in a state of freedom, free from the problems holding you back. This is how I would like you to approach reading this book—with an open mind, one not affected by your current and past anxieties. In later chapters of this book, we will look at how to deal with problems, but for now let's concentrate on the kind of thinking you can use to develop an exciting future.

After you have put aside the lists, take out several more pieces of paper and create answers for the following series of lists. As you do, remember what Sean Covey said about lists: "If all you live by is a daily to-do list, you will simply be managing crises and won't be necessarily accomplishing what matters most."

ASPIRATIONS

1. List your dreams and desires.
2. List what you want to achieve in life.
3. List your future aspirations.
4. List the people you want to be with to share and enjoy your life.
5. List how you want to feel
6. List what you are passionate about.
7. List all the things that could make your future more exciting.

Once again, feel free to add to these lists as they apply to you in particular. The difference in these two lists is obvious. They are two totally different approaches to self-evaluation. One deals with problems, limits—all that infringes on your life—while the other deals with opportunities.

When you put your problems aside, you become free of those negative influences on your life and arrive at a point of freedom—freedom from the negative drain that each of these problems have on your life. Being free of these negative influences will bring you to a point where you can open your mind to exciting possibilities for your future. As we approach opening our imagination, we need to cast aside old prejudices, misconceptions, and negative attitudes. These get in the way of free thinking and open-minded discovery. Anything is possible in your life. Nothing will stand in the way of manifesting your most important dreams and desires. This is the attitude you need to have. But, to adopt this attitude, you need to approach your research and thinking with an open mind, ready to accept all the wonderful opportunities that await you.

As Catherine Pulsifer says, "Opportunities are presented to us each and every day, but do we see them? To see an opportunity, we must be open to all thoughts." You can achieve anything you want. You will become what you constantly think about, and that is why it is so important to open your mind and fill it with positive thoughts that will inspire you to accomplish anything on your achievement list.

As you read through this book, you will discover messages that will inspire you to think deeply about your life, your beliefs and most importantly, your deepest desires. Enjoy the process, enjoy the freedom of thinking clearly and of opening your mind to the possibilities. Most chapters end with a series of questions to answer and lists to complete. These will guide your discovery process.

Take a look at any widely acclaimed scholar, entrepreneur, artist or historical figure. Whether they're formally educated or not, you'll find they are a product of continuous self-education, investing copious amounts of time and energy to improve themselves, which is one of the highest forms of self-love.

—Marc and Angel Chernoff

THINK ABSTRACTLY

Abstraction allows man to see with his mind what he cannot physically see with his eyes. Abstract art enables the artist to perceive beyond the tangible, to extract the infinite out of the finite. It is the emancipation of the mind. It is the explosion into unknown areas.

—Arshile Gorky

When we were in school and taking classes in algebra, analytic geometry or calculus, we were being prepared for abstract thinking. Connecting data to formulas helps us find answers, resolve problems, and understand mathematical relationships. Though it is not often recognized, mathematics is a creative profession, as are so many others where abstract thinking is involved. We often think of creativity only as an artist's or designer's approach to problem-solving. But anyone involved with using their imagination to build something new is involved in the creative process.

When an architect begins the design process, he or she begins by trying to develop a concept that will resolve a problem for their client. The process used is both concrete and abstract. It is like creating the appropriate algebraic equation by taking all the components, information and data and organizing them into a structure that creates the most appropriate solution. The process is organized, but also abstract, and integrates creative concepts with function. As artist Susan Avishai says, "Abstraction demands more from me than realism. Instead of reproducing something outside of me, now I go inward and use everything I've learned thus far in my life."

In fine art, abstract thinking began with the impressionists, with artists like Renoir and Monet who, in their paintings, provided the first generation of abstraction through their impressionistic interpretations of reality. Their looser, painterly techniques did not mimic the reality of those painters of the Renaissance and were the forerunners of what was to come in the art movements of the 20th and 21st centuries. Their impressions of reality led to the more abstract painters of the mid-20th century who created new and much less recognizable impressions of reality. Abstract painters painted what they perceived as an expression of reality and what was in their mind. What is reality? Isn't it one's perception? And if so, then one's perceptions of reality can have many interpretations.

In language, an abstraction is a thought or an idea that does not have a physical or concrete existence. Abstractions are concepts you can't touch or taste–they must be imagined, like love, justice, honor, beauty, freedom, truth, and happiness. Hayakawa, in his 1939 book, *Language in Thought and Action*, said learning is a matter of moving up the ladder from concrete observations toward broader comprehension. Young children live in a world of specifics and learn wider categories and greater abstraction as they grow. As adults, we move easily up and down the ladder from concrete to abstract as the context or message demands. Tom Barrett calls this zooming in or zooming out. There's always a place for the simple facts, but broad concepts are virtually impossible without abstract thought.

In music, composition is an inherently abstract process. Before music is composed and written, there is an empty page, a musical staff without notes or directions. Thinking in an abstract and creative process, the composer harnesses his or her musical vision through the application of well-structured notes in a mathematical pattern that eventually provides the listener with the beautiful relationships and sequences that become a melody. Much like writing a book, the composer structures a score like a musical story, each note something like a word in the sentence, carrying with it the emotions of sound and sound patterns. The musical score must have an outline with various patterns of energy and emotional pitch. Much like the author, the composer has the ability to use time. Unlike the artist painting the canvas, who has one static moment of the viewer's perception, musicians and writers can guide the listener or reader through time, playing with emotion. All of this is framed within a mathematical maze. Without an understanding of mathematics, the writing of music could lose its structural patterns, and the writing of a score could lack focus, direction and balance.

The mixing of logical and abstract thinking is vital to the creative process. As you think about your life, I challenge you to use abstract thinking in your approach to making changes. Try to begin without being influenced by preconceptions and biases. Try to start with a clean slate and approach your future with an expectant attitude. Look deeply at your life and the conditions that help or hurt your progress toward achieving your purpose and reaching your goals. This is your time to enjoy the creative process, imagine the unique possibilities that could be part of your future and design directions that will bring both meaning and excitement to your life. So, speculate, dream, imagine and then gradually validate your decisions with a more concrete analysis.

Think of the development of mathematical formulas for your solutions to problems. Use the creative techniques of the architect, mathematician, designer, musician, and writer to create solutions that are original, developed with a unique approach. Think of other ways of doing things that are stimulated by abstract thinking and work with new and exciting assumptions that can generate more interesting results. Adopt forward thinking to your process. Let the past go and use it only for its positive influence in stimulating your new visions and creative thinking. Build your future by unleashing your imagination with a new spirit of curiosity and by harnessing the potential that abstract thinking can generate.

Thinking—in particular abstract thinking, which most of us are introduced to through the study of mathematics and literature—helps us learn that we can become problem solvers.

—Kathryn Lasky

FOSTER YOUR DREAMS

Every great dream begins with a dreamer. Always remember, you have within you the strength, the patience, and the passion to reach for the stars to change the world.

—Harriet Tubman

What a wonderful activity to engage in – dreaming. Is it just wondering, "what if," is it thinking with a free spirit, or does it extend to speculative planning? As children, we are often criticized for daydreaming. And yet, this is probably where most exciting ideas come from – free thought, unqualified speculation and imagining the possibilities. We all need to spend time in a dream state, whether it is called meditation, yoga, tai chi or any other activity that allows us to escape from the present and go into a state of deep thinking – a state of mindfulness. We need time alone to eliminate the anxieties of the day, where we can generate new ideas and creative approaches to problems, or just a time and space to let the distractions flush from our mind and create a state of mental cleansing.

This could be the answer to stimulating the imagination so vital to the planning process. The more we can free our mind from the problems and distractions of the day, the more we can approach our thinking with originality and clarity. Then we can create. Then we can become original. Then we can plan the life that nourishes our mind and brings excitement to our life. As Gloria Steinem says, "Without leaps of imagination, we lose the excitement of possibilities. Dreaming, after all, is a form of planning."

"There is no way to happiness; happiness is the way," Thich Nhat Hanh says in *The Art of Living*, as he sets the stage for applying your dreams in the present day. He says:

> We have the tendency to think there is a means, a path, to realizing our dream, and that we realize our dream at the end of the path. But in the spirit of Buddhism, as soon as you have a dream, an intention, an ideal, you have to live it. Your dream can be realized right in the present moment. You live your life in such a way that every step in the right direction and every breath along the way becomes the realization of your dream. Your dream does not take you away from the present; on the contrary, your dream becomes reality in the present moment.

Your dreams, just like your happiness, can be part of your daily experience as you realize your entire dream. Integrating your dreams into your daily life will inject a level of excitement and pleasure to encourage you to continue on to reach your ultimate dream. Your dreams are always firmly pictured in your vision, and your dreams are always within you.

Throughout our formal education, we have been trained to learn processes, facts and vital information that are key to understanding our field of study in depth. We learn what is known, what has been scientifically verified, and what the standard practices are within our field of study. But what we don't learn is how to create what doesn't exist. And that is the future.

The future is formed by our imagination, our dreams and by putting the past aside to use only as a reference in formulating our future. We need to erase the clutter and free ourselves to make changes with an open mind, a creative mind, a mind free of the routines, habits and patterns of the past. We need to free ourselves to let our dreams surface; they can guide us through the abstract maze of the future.

We need dreams. We need to dream. This is what stimulates the imaginative spirit within us.

Consult not your fears but your hopes and your dreams. Think not about your frustrations, but about your unfulfilled potential. Concern yourself not with what you tried and failed in, but with what it is still possible for you to do.

—Pope John XXIII

DREAM BIG

Desire is the starting point of all achievement, not a hope, not a wish, but a keen pulsating desire which transcends everything.

—Napoleon Hill

Having worked in the advertising business most of my life, I know that creating desire for a product or service is part of the selling process. As the AIDA formula goes, first we need to attract

Attention; then we need to develop
Interest; third, we need to instill
Desire; and fourth, we need to provide a path for
Action.

These words have been the cornerstone of advertising strategy for decades, and all are part of the process of persuading customers to buy products. When enough interest is built up about a specific product, it becomes a desire: we are hooked. No matter what the rationale, no matter what the data shows, if we love it and have a heightened desire for that product, we will buy it.

What do you desire – an antique automobile, advancement in your profession, a wonderful vacation to Europe, or a more in-depth relationship with a special person? You have been thinking about it for months, even years. Every time you see it driving down the road or in a magazine advertisement, your desire is intensified until finally you make the move: you decide to buy it or make that call to get the process started.

Desires are great. They are what get you excited about life. They are what you think about a lot of the time and, when you act on them, they can move you toward a more exciting life. Let your desires come out. Let them surface and act as a stimulus for taking action. It has been said that as we reflect on life in our final days on this Earth, we are more disappointed about what we didn't do in life than pleased about what we did do. It doesn't have to be this way. Don't live with regrets. It's not too late. Bring your desires into reality by taking action and making the decision to jump in headfirst and fulfill those dreams and desires that have been on your mind for so many decades. As Confucius says, "The will to win, the desire to succeed, the urge to reach your full potential… These are the keys to personal excellence."

Having desires enriches your life and reinforces your optimism. They can be what you look forward to doing, enjoying, or achieving. Desires may have built up so that you can actually feel as if you have attained your wishes. A dream and a desire are closely linked. A dream is the initial stage of wanting something, but a desire is close to passion. How can your desires help you chart a course for developing a more exciting life? What first steps could you take to test the waters of your desires to see if they could become a reality? How would you feel when you reach the point when your desires have manifested into a reality?

Your life is your life. It's driven by your wishes and aspirations, all of which are unique to you. Why not harness those desires and let them influence your actions? Big goals come from big dreams. When big dreams become specific, recognized desires, great things can happen to your life. Exciting new adventures will evolve, and your level of enthusiasm and appreciation for life will explode. Enjoy the process. Let those desires take hold of your decisions and reach a unique new level of living that will open the door to a vast array of new and exciting experiences.

Intense, burning desire is the motivational force that enables you to overcome any obstacle and achieve almost any goal.

—Brian Tracy

ENCOURAGE YOUR CURIOSITY

We keep moving forward, opening new doors, and doing new things, because we're curious and curiosity keeps leading us down new paths.

—Walt Disney

The truth is not yet totally known. We live in an ever-changing world where assumptions and theories are challenged on a daily basis. Science continues to find new evidence about our world, our origins and everything around us. We continue to grow in our understanding and discover things we never even knew existed before. And today we face paradigm-changing advances, like artificial intelligence and virtual reality.

Such advances often make us question our beliefs, and if they don't, they should. It is very easy to be stuck in our thinking, our assumptions, our long-standing concepts of life and how we live it. We must embrace the continuing research and curiosity of our inventive professionals in every field of study. We do not know everything yet, and we need to give curiosity a chance and support the imaginative and innovative pursuits that bring about advancements in our understanding of our world and of our lives. "No one is dumb who is curious," says Neil deGrasse Tyson. "The people who don't ask questions remain clueless throughout their lives."

WHAT IS, ISN'T

What is good enough for today, is not necessarily true for tomorrow, or next month or next year. So why hold on to traditions and assumptions that have been gathering dust for decades? Curiosity stimulates the imagination and inspires us to ask how and why. Our imagination brings us closer to invention and innovation. Curiosity is one of the most powerful forces influencing our thinking. It makes us see things in a different way and encourages creativity and new approaches to everyday situations in need of change, advancement, and improvement. Curiosity, imagination, innovation, improvement, and change – these advance our society and can advance our personal lives. In the words of Albert Einstein: "I have no special talent. I am only passionately curious." Or as Elizabeth Gilbert says, in *Big Magic*,

> You might spend your whole life following your curiosity and have absolutely nothing to show for it at the end – except one thing. You will have the satisfaction of knowing that you passed your entire existence in devotion to the noble human virtue of inquisitiveness. And that should be more than enough for anyone to say that they lived a rich and splendid life.

Curiosity inspires growth – mental growth. That's a good reason to continue asking questions, to continue trying to understand "why." Curiosity nourishes our mind, stimulates our creativity and allows us to investigate new directions for our life.

KEEP ASKING QUESTIONS

Keep asking why. And seek to understand all the basic truths that are part of your belief structure. What will come next? What new inventions will change your life and the way the world works? These are the exciting questions that we must continue to ask. Not everything is known yet. So, open your mind to the possibilities, to the unknown and imagine what could be. Imagine what is not here yet. Anything is possible, and through the unleashing of your imagination, anything can be created.

My favorite words are possibilities, opportunities and curiosity. I think if you are curious, you create opportunities, and then if you open the doors, you create possibilities.

—Mario Testino

DAYDREAM

If you don't daydream and kind of plan things out in your imagination, you never get there. So you have to start someplace.

—Robert Duvall

Daytime is a great time to dream. We are fully conscious, aware of our surroundings, and ready to document our thoughts on paper or computer for later reference. Dreaming at night is much less useful. First, it is governed by our subconscious, often confusing, and almost always difficult to remember. And in a night dream you are not able to integrate your conscious thoughts and bring about new and exciting conclusions to your thinking. And, of course, you can't take out a tablet of paper and pen and write down those thoughts when you are in a deep state of sleep.

We all live in a fantasy world. We must. We are all unique. We see things differently. In fact, we can look at the same object or scene and each of us perceive it differently. Our perceptions are formed by our prejudices, and our prejudices are built on a lifetime of experiences. These experiences are naturally different for everyone. Consequently, we see things differently from anyone else even when we are looking at the same object. Hence, we live in our own world. I like to think of it as our own fantasy world. Each one of us is unique, and each one of our worlds is unique. We see, listen, smell, taste, and feel through the perceptions we have inherited or shaped. And each one of our senses is influenced by our own unique experiences. We live in a fantasy of our own making, built by our own perceptions and convictions.

In the words of Daniel Goleman, "Daydreaming incubates creative discovery." If we are to harness our creative energies, we must start by expanding our imagination in a dream state. Consider doing it at a time that allows our imagination to be most effective – dreaming during the day. As children, we are often discouraged from daydreaming. It is considered a foolish distraction, especially when we should be listening to the teacher. But discouraging young people from nurturing their imagination through dreaming is working against innovative thinking and against a most rewarding experience. To dream, we must start with a clear and open mind, cast aside our preconceptions, and begin to imagine the possibilities. We must live in the present and not in the past—the present is all we have! Possibilities and opportunities lie only in the future. They are there waiting for us to use and integrate into our lives.

Daydreaming is the starting point for creating a new life or redesigning a business: it is an imperative step to unleashing the creative spirit within. Ralph Lauren says, "I don't design clothes, I design dreams."

So, close the door, turn on your favorite Bach piano concerto, put yourself in an unencumbered place of rest, and daydream. Start the process of building a new future that only you can imagine. Let daydreaming open the door to your new and exciting future.

I'm not much of a math and science guy. I spent most of my time in school daydreaming and managed to turn it into a living.

—George Lucas

IMAGINE THE POSSIBILITIES

Then we send kids to school, and that fantastic creative process is suddenly a bad thing. The child's imagination is called 'not paying attention.' Drifting off into the glorious realm of the imagination for a few moments elicits a swift 'What are you doing?!' from the teacher.

—Bob Procter

The more imaginative you are, the more creative you will be, and the more creative you are, the more possibilities unfold for an exciting, innovative, passionate, and dynamic life. This is why I titled this book *Unleash Your Imagination*. We are obsessed with making out lists, setting goals and prioritizing to achieve these goals. And yet, often these goals have not been formulated by reaching deep inside and stretching our imagination to achieve a list of truly spectacular goals, goals that ignite our passions, our dreams and all that allows our fantasies to surface and influence our desires. Does this sound impossible? Perhaps. But why limit yourself when you are trying to unleash the dreams that are hidden within you? According to Albert Einstein, "Imagination is more important than knowledge."

Can you imagine the possibilities? What if you could realize the dreams of long ago that never came to fruition? What if you could live in that cottage by the ocean and hear the seagulls calling? What if you could spend a year living in the south of France and experience the charm of the Mediterranean coast and be influenced by the light and the atmosphere that inspired the impressionist painters? What if you could live with those who reinforce your life and inspire you to reach for new, far-reaching goals well beyond what you thought you could achieve? What if you could live with the expectation that a spectacular life is possible?

But when you do set goals, don't set simple goals—goals that you know you can achieve. Those are not much more than a Saturday morning laundry list. Set goals that you have no idea how you can achieve. Stretch so far that you enter a world of spectacular possibilities. Set goals that create excitement in your life and allow you to anticipate their reality. In his book, *The Art of Living*, Bob Proctor says: "If you set a goal and you know how to achieve it, you're not growing. You're going sideways. When you set a goal, you should be setting a goal for something you have absolutely no idea how to do." You may never reach such a goal, but you will have stretched your imagination so far that it will take you much further than you thought you could go. You will have achieved even higher levels of discovery along the way. In *The Law of Attraction,* Esther and Jerry Hicks say,

> Imagination is the mixing and massaging of thoughts into various combinations. It is similar to observing a situation. However, in imagination, you are creating the images rather than watching something in your current reality. Some use the word visualization, but we want to offer this subtle distinction: *Visualization* is often only a memory of something that you have once observed. By *imagination,* we mean deliberately bringing desired components together in your mind to create a desired scenario…When we use the term imagination, we are really talking about *Deliberately Creating* your own reality.

Unleash your imagination. Re-imagine your future. Think of the spectacular possibilities. They are there waiting for you. You control your life. You are responsible for the decisions that guide your future, and you have free rein to make it happen. It begins with unleashing your imagination.

There is hope in dreams, imagination and in the courage of those who wish to make those dreams a reality.

—Jonas Salk

MATERIALIZE YOUR WISHES

Don't leave your life up to chance. Grab the reins of your life, and charge gallantly in the direction of your grandest vision.

—Darren Hardy

What gives you hope for the future? What makes you excited about the next phase in your life? Wishes are the undercurrent of your motivation. They stimulate your desire to live a more exciting future. Look deeply into your wishes. They are important in your life and are a result of your desires and a lifetime of experiences.

Do you remember your first birthday cake and the thrill of making the first wish and knowing that it would come true if you blew out all the candles? It was an exciting experience. And at age 30, 50 or 85, we are still making a birthday wish and hoping for great results. That is great, because wishes are crucial for looking to the future with hope and enthusiasm. Encourage your imagination to make out a list of as many wishes as you can and know that having the wish is the first step to making it come true.

Wishes are important at every phase of life. Just because we are older doesn't mean that tomorrow is not just as important as it was at an earlier stage in our life. Being older makes every remaining day more precious. Wishes shape every tomorrow. They forecast a better day tomorrow and in the future. And who doesn't want a better future?

Approach wishes with optimism. The more optimistic you are about your wishes, the more you will enable them to come to life. Our lives can be filled with the results of our wishes. Encourage them. Let them surface. Think of how thrilling your life will be when your wishes are realized.

We all have our own life to pursue, our own kind of dream to be weaving, and we all have the power to make wishes come true, as long as we keep believing.

—Louisa May Alcott

t w o

UNLEASH YOUR FANTASIES

LIVE YOUR FANTASY

The gift of fantasy has meant more to me than my talent for absorbing positive knowledge.

—Albert Einstein

HAVE YOU EVER HAD A FRIEND SAY, "Have a fantastic day?" Of course, you've heard that. But what does it mean? I always thought of it as the equivalent of "Have a great day" or "Have a wonderful day." But when we look more closely, we see the word "fantasy embedded. And "fantasy" can mean, "creative imagination; unrestrained fancy" and "a creation of the fancy," or "an unrealistic or improbable supposition." Another definition suggests "highly fanciful or supernatural elements." So, the next time you say, "Have a fantastic day!", you could be suggesting to your friend "have a creative, unrestrained, unrealistic and supernatural day." That would open up some concerns about your relationship!

Actually, fantasy and fantasizing are wonderful concepts. A fantasy can be a place or a journey or an adventure that takes you in an unrestrained manner to a dream world or place that embodies all your wishes and desires. And, of course, that is what we're talking about here. Let's not follow the traditional avenues. Let's open our minds to fantasy. You don't have to act on it, but you can set the scene by expanding your imagination to a place that is exciting and fulfills all your dreams.

I am impressed with how Ferdinand Porsche realized his fantasy and found a solution: "I couldn't find the sports car of my dreams, so I built it myself." This simple but powerful statement shows how we not only need to develop our fantasies, but also to bring them into reality. Many authors say you need to visualize your preferred future. They urge you to visualize a place where you would like to be, something you would like to have accomplished, or a person you would like to be with. In other words, visualize your fantasy.

A fantasy is an unleashed vision, unrestrained by any roadblocks and open to creative thinking. Often, "fantasies" are connected with make-believe places like we might see in sci fi movies or movies with comic book heroes, in a past distorted by nostalgia or a future shaped by wishful thinking or dread. But fantasies can also be the origins of your dreams and aspirations. If we start our search with unrestrained fantasy as we create our vision, we allow ourselves to exercise our imagination to discover those subconscious desires, allow our dreams to surface and put us on track to experience something very new in our lives. Fantasy has the potential for creating some very exciting changes in our lives.

Making slight adjustments to your current situation will do just that – make slight adjustments to your potential. Slight adjustments make small changes. To be able to really supercharge your life, you need big shifts, big dreams, big aspirations, and that takes creative thinking. Visualize your fantasies. Make them seem real. Then detail them out with your imagination. Just think of the possibilities, the excitement, and the exceptional life that you could be creating.

Whether or not you are aware of it, deep in your heart there is something you've always wanted to accomplish. Not just a fleeting wish but a deep intention that may have begun to grow in your heart while you were still very young. This is your dearest dream, your ultimate concern. When you identify and nurture your deepest desire, it can become a source of great happiness, energy, and motivation. It can provide you with drive, with direction. It can sustain you through difficult moments.

—Thich Nhat Hanh

NURTURE YOUR OBSESSIONS

I've been called many names like perfectionist, difficult and obsessive. I think it takes obsession, takes searching for the details for any artist to be good.

—Barbra Streisand

We often hear that a balanced life is a good life. By giving equal emphasis to the seven major categories in our life requires us to devote at least some minimal attention to each area. When nothing is overlooked, we can keep things on an even keel. However, while a well-balanced life is seen as mentally healthy, it does not allow for a dramatic thrust into a direction that may be extremely important to us. Only by unbalancing our lives and emphasizing those things that are important to us, can we make significant accomplishments.

Let's look at the seven main categories in life that need constant attention. We can title them in a variety of ways, but they come down to these categories: family, professional, health, financial, spiritual, personal, and cultural. Place them into a chart or diagram and give them a value or percentage of time that you wish to dedicate to each one. For a balanced life, your chart might look something like this:

Balanced Life	Time Allotted
Family	15%
Professional	15%
Health	15%
Financial	15%
Spiritual	15%
Personal	15%
Cultural	10%

In this concept of a well-balanced life, almost everything is given nearly equal attention. Each area of life is supported with our time and efforts. However, this might describe a life that is too much in balance. If nothing has been given significance or importance, this can, unfortunately, lead to a life with little impact: a little bit here and a little bit there, with no dramatic emphasis. Balance might be good for an acrobat or a person who wants to lead a peaceful life, but it is disastrous if you want big accomplishments. What is missing in a balanced life is the burning desire so important to the happiness of an achievement-oriented person. If a person has a burning desire to make a major accomplishment, the percentages might look like this:

Achievement-Oriented Life	Time Allotted
Family	10%
Professional	50%
Health	5%
Financial	10%
Spiritual	5%
Personal	10%
Cultural	10%

There are only twenty-four hours in a day, so the percentages must add up to 100%. This means we must steal time from other categories to dedicate significant time to a major project. Does this unbalance our life? Yes, it probably does; however, with 50% of the available time dedicated to a significant professional project, it might also be a formula for success. How can we rationalize creating this type of imbalance in our lives? We can do it by dedicating ourselves to a cause or to approaching a dynamic idea with a healthy obsession. Such extreme passion is essential when we need to work on its solution until it is completed. We need to be preoccupied with our cause, our idea, or our project. Commitment like this gives a project a position of prime importance in our life.

Did the doctors and nurses and all the first responders during the Covid-19 pandemic live a balanced life? Did they work a forty-hour week, eight to five, and then go home to be with their family? No. They worked until the job was done, until all the patients were cared for and only when exhaustion set in, did they consider leaving for the day. They were dedicated to caring for their patients, and they knew their families would understand and support them. What drives researchers to work until all hours of the night to continue with their investigation and experimentation? It is their commitment to finding an answer. What drives teachers to hold classes throughout the day, come home at night, grade papers, and prepare the assignments for the next day? It is their passion for helping young students, stimulating their minds, and improving their lives. Think of the author writing a book, the musician composing a musical score, the entrepreneur starting a new business, the student pursuing a college degree. All have a healthy obsession with creating, learning, and building something that will make a major contribution to our society.

Being driven by a healthy obsession is essential to great success. We need to be dedicated to a cause to commit the time and effort required to accomplish the tasks necessary to our work. As you think about your life, select your cause, feel your mission, purpose, and obsession, and plan your time accordingly as you allocate a percentage of time to each category of your life. Realize that you can't do everything; there is only so much time available to each of us. By making this decision, you will enhance your ability to pursue your passion. You will know that you have the time to research, create, experiment, and accomplish what is important to you.

Color is my daylong obsession, joy, and torment.

—Claude Monet

FIND YOUR DEEPEST DESIRE

Dreams help us imagine our lives as dramas that once again present the eternal journeys, longings, and struggles that define every human life.

—Thomas Moore

What is the one thing that motivates you, excites you and makes you jump out of bed in the morning ready to start another wonderful day? In

The One Thing, Gary Keller and Jay Papasan help their readers identify the most important thing that needs to be addressed in order to help them achieve their goals. Is there one thing? There may be several important things that need resolution in some manner. Many of these things may be important and in need of serious consideration. But of all these things, one may surface as the most critical, as the one that stands in the way of making progress or as the one that will unleash your imagination and help you develop a plan to create an exceptional life.

Confronting the "one thing" usually involves identifying the most important obstacle in the way of your making progress toward reaching your goals. This might be improving your health, paying off a major debt, returning to school to study for an advanced degree or getting certification in your profession. All kinds of things can threaten your security and hold you back from achieving your goals. Such things might be standing in the way of reaching the next level in your profession. But there is something more important than obstacles: the many opportunities for shaping your desired future. But what do you really want? What do you really want to choose for your life?

It is crucial to understand who we are, to dig deep and figure out who we are, why we exist, what our purpose is in life, what values we hold as the most important, and what influences our decisions. How do those values help set our goals, make contributions to our community and world, and influence our hope of leaving a legacy? In *How, Then, Shall We Live*, Wayne Muller poses four questions:

1. Who am I?
2. What do I love?
3. How shall I live, knowing I will die?
4. What is my gift to the family of the Earth?

These questions can lead you to a better understanding of who you are.

One process that can be used to understand who we are is to understand our current situation. Often this means making a list of our problems, the people who are stopping us from moving forward, and all of the obstacles in our way. This might be a great way to identify all of our problems, but it can have a grim outcome. Spending a day wrestling with our problems can be a depressing activity and might not lead to good results. However, what if we approach these issues from a totally different perspective? What if we start with a blank sheet of paper and see the future as an open opportunity to create a life that is wonderful, reinforcing, and exciting? What if we, from the start, intentionally put our problems aside and investigate the tremendous opportunities before us?

Starting with a blank sheet, we can unleash our desires and passions and start to plan a beautiful life. Problems can hold us back, but dreaming can provide the excitement that prompts us to see an exceptional vision of our future. It allows us to see our potential and clarify our desires. How do we approach this blank sheet? What do you want to find out? Asking the right questions will help us identify the best answers. I suggest starting with the following lists:

A VISION OF MY EXCEPTIONAL FUTURE

1. What do I value? For example, we can see from Mozart's exceptional life that he loved music; and from this, we can deduce that one of his values was beauty, the beauty of music.
2. What do I believe?
3. What are my hopes?
4. What are my dreams and desires?
5. How do I want to feel?
6. What do I want to achieve?

Develop every list with a positive and optimistic objective. This is not time to be swayed by negativity. We want to dream of a fantastic future and use every resource to make that future become a reality.

Many of us use lists at the beginning of the day or weekend that I will call a "Saturday morning to-do list." To exist in a settled life, we need these lists: mow the grass, wash the clothes, get the car serviced and shop for food. These are important to keeping our life in balance, but such tasks are at a very low level in our total life plan. It is important to add two more lists to be able to evaluate our life and set new goals: A List of Achievements and a List of Feelings. How you want to feel is the most important realization for achieving a happy and joyful life. Let me recommend the following order of list making:

1. Make a list of how you want to feel.
2. Make a list of what you want to achieve to support your desired feelings.
3. Make a list of the action steps it will take to implement these.

Now things are in proper order. Start with your desired feelings and then determine what it will take to achieve those feelings, as in this example:

1. I want to feel intellectually stimulated (feelings list)
2. I want to write a book about 15th century Italian architecture (achievement list)
3. Contact a travel agent to plan my itinerary in Italy (to-do list)

When all of your to-do's are based on your desired feelings and achievements, you are on course to make your daily activities and to-do's meaningful and purposeful. In the end, you will have worked in a congruent manner where your beliefs and feeling are aligned with your actions. Start with your feelings. Start with your desired future. During this process you will find that your deepest desire will begin to surface. This is the one thing that will inspire you to reach your preferred future, and it will be based on your deepest wishes, dreams and desires.

The will to win, the desire to succeed, the urge to reach your full potential…these are the keys that will unlock the door to personal excellence.

—Confucius

FOCUS / UN-FOCUS

Abstract thinking leads to greater creativity...But in our business and our life, we often do the opposite. We intensify our focus rather than widen our view.

—Daniel Pink

Focusing has its appropriate moment in the design development process, but that at the origins of creating a product, a solution to a problem or a new concept, we need to un-focus to open our mind to a full range of possibilities. In his book *Tinker, Dabble, Doodle, Try: Unlock the Power of the Unfocused Mind,* Srini Pillay says, "The conventional line of thinking is that the ability to focus is the key to getting things done. ... But allowing our minds to wander can actually increase our productivity." Many books about life planning and business success have one central theme – focusing. To solve problems, we need to understand the criteria and influences that create the problems and nourish their continuation, and only then can we focus on the evaluation processes. This is called focusing on the path to problem resolution. This process works well as long as we have a clear understanding of the facts and everything that created the problem in the first place. But it channels us into a conservative process that limits our ability to think with originality or find a fresh, imaginative approach to a resolution.

In contrast, artist Joseph Plaskett says,

> I had always made pictures as I thought I saw the world, focusing on what lay in front, but this is not how one sees the world. It only frames the centre and cuts off the lateral vision, which lies unfocused. Now I found that I could turn my eyes to the adjacent field of vision, seeing another focus, an extension which I added to the original. Instead of stopping at two focuses, I looked further to the side, adding another and yet another.

I would suggest that you give yourself a chance to un-focus. Facts are important, and analysis is essential, but they do not always lead us to the answer. We often ask the wrong questions and therefore seek the wrong solutions. Beginning with an analytical process of problem-solving can channel us toward an unimaginative resolution. Let's start with, not only thinking out of the box, but thinking with originality. Let's ask questions that may not have been asked before. Let's approach the problem from a vastly different point of view. Let's un-focus and see what results we can achieve. Consider creative processes like mind-mapping, storyboarding and stream of consciousness thinking where ideas can flow without limitation or preconceptions. Speculate on different end results than what you have been imagining. Avoid the mental trap of inadequate alternatives – thinking "Should I do this or that?" – and consider multiple possibilities instead.

Frame your questions in original and inventive ways that promote innovative thinking and solutions. This is un-focusing, and it places us in a different space than might be typical. Working from a freer point of view allows us to see new solutions, new answers, and new pathways without being inhibited by standard assumptions and rote processes. Open your mind, allow your imagination to flourish, and see what happens.

Scientists know they must not "begin with the end in mind" but follow the facts and accept the results of experiments even when these are surprising or disappointing. But this is hard. Scientists have to learn to do this, and history is littered with examples of their failure to do so. That's because we all tend to do our research in reverse order. We choose a solution and then try to defend it though our research and discovery process. What we need to do is begin our research with an open mind, without preselecting the results. This leaves us open to many solutions, many avenues of resolution. When we are not locked into a predetermined answer, we are able to discover a variety of inventive solutions to our problem. So, start with fully understanding the details of the problem. Ask why it is a problem and determine what has encouraged the problem to exist. Then, when you have a firm grasp on the nature of the problem, you can proceed with your research, knowing that the potential answers will be unaffected by preconceptions.

Marcel Proust says, "The voyage of discovery is not in seeking new landscapes but in having new eyes." How can this be done? Imagine opening your eyes in the morning and seeing the world from another person's point of view. Imagine seeing the world from the eyes and minds of Pablo Picasso, Frank Lloyd Wright, or Henry David Thoreau. What would the world look like? What would be your perception through the eyes of Wright? What would become important? What would be highlighted to you as never before? I consider this to be good practice in un-focusing– intentionally not seeing as you would normally see, but seeing from another point of view, from another mind, from another set of priorities. Imagine purchasing a pair of glasses that would automatically change your vision as if you were seeing through another person's eyes, driven by another person's mind. Hear the words of Mark Twain when he says, "You can't depend on your eyes when your imagination is out of focus."

Life stretches out for miles all around you. Once you are no longer blinded by your own plans and projects, a fascinating world shows up, just waiting for you to open your eyes and see it.

—Barbara Sher

WATER THE FLOWERS

When things aren't adding up in our life, start subtracting. Life gets easier when you delete the things and people that make it difficult. Get rid of some of life's complexities so you can spend more time with people you love and do more of the things you love. This means getting rid of the physical clutter and eliminating all but the essential, so you are left with only the things that give you value.

—Marc and Angel Chernoff

To find the inner peace that allows you to reach your personal point of freedom, it's important to reduce the negative impact that people and things have on your life.

Long ago, I attended the Aspen Design Conference in Colorado. Many prominent designers, educators and civic leaders were there, among them, Leopold Kohr. Along with Jonas Salk, Milton Glaser, and Saul Bass, he was one of the primary speakers at the Conference. The premise of Kohr's presentation followed his philosophy—the reason for all problems in the world is "bigness" and that the size of the problems we face is directly related to how seriously they impact our lives. He says, "Bigness, or oversize, is really much more than just a social misery. It appears to be the one and only problem permeating all creation…Whenever something is wrong, something is too big."

When a problem is small it may be inconsequential and can probably be overlooked – it is not significant enough to be important. If we can reduce the size of the problems that confront us, they can become of little importance.

In *Getting Back to Happy,* Marc and Angel Chernoff speak directly to the concept of reducing the clutter in our lives so that we interact only with things and people that bring value. We need to do this to achieve our most important goals. We need to get rid of the things that stand in the way of reaching these goals. By uncluttering our lives, we can find the inner peace and balance that inspires joy and happiness. To get to this point in our lives, we need to separate ourselves from the distractions of our daily routines and move to a place where we can think more clearly and contemplate our future.

Contemplation, self-introspection, and perhaps even meditation can be techniques for separating yourself from the turmoil of daily life. To do this, find a quiet place—a place of solitude—away from the complexity of routines and constant interruptions, where you can think, dream and imagine the possibilities. We have in our mind decades of information and ideas to rely on, if only we could quiet the noise around us and draw on that information and those memories. All this information can be the beginning of new directions for our lives and offer the potential for change from the monotonous routines that bog us all down.

To make a change, we need to get rid of the influence of daily rituals that overshadow our imagination and creativity with unimportant details. We need to make choices that free us from routines and allow us to create new daily patterns that reinforce innovative thinking and allow us to seek new opportunities. Close the door. Get quiet. Imagine. Think. Dream. And enjoy the world of your imagination. You are the person who will reap the rewards of your imaginative thinking. So, find that place and contemplate your life and your current reality. Begin to dream about your vision for your future.

As you begin the process of contemplating your life and your future, think of your mind as being a storage space filled with small compartments. Each of these compartments is individually filled with ideas, memories, experiences, and all kinds of information. Now imagine that to introduce new compartments with new ideas, you had to empty some of the old ones to make room for the new ones. Are there compartments that contain old ideas which have a negative impact on your ability to be creative? Are there compartments filled with memories that are negative influences on you and make you say no to your new desires? I'm sure there are. As you evaluate each of your mental compartments, make out a list of those ideas, influences and people who are inhibiting you from advancing in new directions. These are the things to remove and discard because they are getting in your way. Don't make excuses and think that you cannot allow yourself to imagine a new future. You have every right to do so; in fact, it is your responsibility to create a life that uses every iota of your creativity and potential.

Don't let anything get in the way of your success. Don't blame anyone else. You are in control. You are the person who will create your new life and make it happen. As the Chernoffs say,

> All education is self-education. It doesn't matter if you're sitting in a college classroom or a coffee shop. We don't learn anything we don't want to learn. Those who take the time and initiative to pursue knowledge on their own are the only ones who earn a real education in this world.

Just think how important that statement is and what it means to you. You are responsible for understanding yourself and your current reality.

The more you trust and believe in your potential and approach your research in an open-minded and honest manner, the deeper you will search to unearth the truth about yourself and the more you will enable yourself to find the paths to freedom from your current situation. In *Big Magic*, Elizabeth Gilbert says, "your education isn't over when they say it's over; your education is over when you say it's over." She also says,

> No matter how great your teachers may be, and no matter how esteemed your academy's reputation, eventually you will have to do the work by yourself. Eventually, the teachers won't be there anymore. The walls of the school will fall away, and you'll be on your own. The hours that you will then put into practice, study, auditions, and creation will be entirely up to you. The sooner and more passionately you get married to this idea – that it is ultimately entirely up to you—the better off you'll be.

Just as the mind is filled with small compartments of thoughts and ideas, we fill life with similar compartments that can overwhelm the time we have available. Only so much can fit into a day, a week, a year or a life. We need to make thoughtful choices as we decide what to place in our life. As you begin to rebuild your life and imagine what it could be, think of your life as an empty space. Borrow a trick from interior designers and take everything out first, at least in your imagination. Imagine your "room" empty, so you can see the space you have to work with. Then begin to fill it with only those things, places and people who positively influence your dreams and aspirations. Don't place anything in that space that negatively impacts your thinking or your plans. Instead, carefully position all those things that will act as a support structure for you as you begin implementing your plans.

Try this exercise: draw a large rectangle on a piece of paper. This is your new space—your new life. Now write the words and draw the images that you want in your new life within the rectangle. By doing this you can begin to develop a visual picture of this new space. Eventually, you will be able to make connections and establish priorities as you see how many of these words and pictures relate to each other and begin to reinforce your future plans.

There are many ways to find a place to experience solitude and to contemplate your life. Thoreau might visit the woods to find peace, Frank Lloyd Wright would find his influence from nature, and some might use meditation techniques. In *Stress Less, Accomplish More: Meditation for Extraordinary Performance,* Emily Fletcher defines three levels of self-reflection: "Mindfulness helps you deal with stress in the present; meditation gets rid of stress from the past; and manifesting helps you clarify your dreams for the future." Whether you find your space in nature or in a quiet room, the experience of self-reflection and of being quiet will help you listen to your inner voice without distraction and allow you to be unencumbered by the distractions of your current reality. Find that space. Find your inner voice. Contemplate your past, present and future and experience excitement and joy in the possibilities of making important changes.

Water the flowers, not the weeds.

—Emily Fletcher

DECIDE WHAT TO SEE

Just make a decision that you will look for what you want to see. It is not a difficult decision to make, but it can make a big difference in what you bring into your experience.

—Esther and Jerry Hicks

Open your eyes to beauty. Open your mind to fantastic opportunities. What do you see when you open your eyes? Problems, distractions, work that needs to be done? Close your eyes and try again. Our eyes, being one of our most important senses, are the gateway to our mind. What we see is what influences our thinking, what sets our mood for the day, and what controls our decision-making. However, we have the ability to choose what we see. We are the editors of our vision, just like we are the designers of our life. We need to capture the mind of the editor or the curator and begin to qualify what we allow to enter our world.

Open your eyes to those visions that will reinforce your values and beliefs. Qualify the images that influence your thinking. You have the capacity and the right to decide how you want to feel. Make that decision first, and see how it can influence what you see. We've all heard the saying, "Seeing is believing." And more recently that has been reversed: "Believing is seeing." I firmly believe that the second quote is on the right track, although not completely accurate.

Many authors talk about optimism and how to live life with an optimistic spirit. Living life with optimism and a positive attitude is essential to being able to control your vision and edit the things you are seeing. Fill your life with those things that are reinforcing and supportive of your values, principles and especially your goals. Believing is seeing. Your beliefs will guide what you are seeing and will help you differentiate the positive from the negative. Seeing can reinforce believing, but be careful what you allow yourself to see. If your beliefs are not strong enough, solid enough, the things that you see will have a strong influence on your beliefs. This is backward thinking.

"Know thyself," the words of Socrates, are more important now than it has ever been, because more things grab for our attention than ever. Consequently, it is critical to make thoughtful choices. What do we listen to? What do we watch? What do we read? We make these choices, and our choices are based on our values and beliefs. So, before we open our eyes, understand the process that governs our thinking.

1. Our feelings inspire our values.
2. Our values influence our beliefs.
3. Our beliefs help establish our principles.
4. Our principles help to form our philosophy.
5. Our philosophy shapes our purpose.
6. Our purpose helps determine our mission.
7. Our mission helps to establish our goals.

8. Our goals govern our actions.

So, what do we do first, feel or see? If we just see, then we are controlled by everything and everyone who wants to influence us. It is unqualified seeing. However, if first, we know how we want to feel, we then can make the appropriate decisions regarding what we want to see and what we want to avoid. How you want to feel governs your beliefs, your values, and your principles, and shapes the manner in which you edit your process of visual selection.

I will step into the field of all possibilities and anticipate the excitement that can occur when I remain open to infinite choices. When I step into the field of all possibilities, I will experience all the fun, adventure, magic, and mystery of life.

—Deepak Chopra

WAKE UP

Waking up is the first act. One day something in you stirs and you wake up from ignorance and sheer unconsciousness. You wake up from neglect of things that matter. You wake up to a new vision of your world and your place in it. You wake up many times during your lifetime, if you're lucky, and never stop waking as you make new significant discoveries.

—Thomas Moore

In *A Religion of One's Own,* Thomas Moore writes about being really awake. To what level? Are we constantly in a state of unconsciousness? Do we follow the routines of our daily life without really thinking? The key to being really awake is to reach a level of enlightenment. Life can be seen in three phases: The Learning Phase, The Productive Phase, and the Enlightenment Phase. We spend the first third of our lives in education, as learners—learning how to ride a bicycle, learning the multiplication tables, learning how to write with precision and clarity, and learning the processes and details of our chosen profession. This is a significant part of our life, and the more we can deposit into our mind, the more we will have to bank on for future decisions.

Second is the Productive Phase, where we harness the learning that we have done and the life experiences that we have had and apply them to our homes, social circles, marriages, children, and careers. This is another long period of life, encompassing, perhaps, the second third of life. Our working years are when our talents and abilities and our professional goals coalesce to contribute to making our mark in the world.

But then there comes the most exciting part of life—the enlightenment phase. With the continuous learning that occurs throughout life and with all of the experiences that we have had, we have developed a storehouse of information to use in defining that last third of our life. We have reached a point of new freedom—freedom from time schedules, deadlines, and constant responsibilities. Often, we are emotionally freer as well. We have raised our children, accomplished many professional goals, accumulated a nest egg (of whatever size!), and learned to stop worrying about some things. This is the enlightenment phase of life, a time to reflect, evaluate, establish new goals, and approach them with knowledge, experience, and dedication. It's an exciting period of life.

So many people see this last phase of life as a time to relax and retire from the responsibilities of the working life. And for many, this may be a needed time of rest and re-cooperation from a hard, working life. But the time will come when you need to experience the awakening Moore describes and discover that you have the last third of your life to live. It can be as long as your entire working career, perhaps twenty, thirty or forty years. This is no time just to sit back in the recliner and relax. It is a time in life to determine how you can use your talents, knowledge, and experience to make your mark on the world, make a contribution to society and leave a legacy to your family, to your profession, and to future generations. We all have causes we are dedicated to, and this is a time to plan a course of action that will allow you to harness your experience to contribute to your cause.

We all face challenges in our lives, and we need to confront those challenges. But most of us in the enlightenment phase will have an enormous amount of time available to extend our professional experience and make a difference. What could this involve? Perhaps providing leadership at a youth camp, giving lectures about something we know well, designing a beautiful garden, or developing a plan for world travel. Or maybe it's time to learn something new, uncover new talents or recover old ones that could enrich our life and the lives of others.

Waking up with enlightenment does not need to arrive in the last third of your life, however. It can happen any time in your life and is most likely during times of change. It could happen upon graduation from college, mid-career changes, when your children leave home or enter college or when you divorce or lose a job. The directions in your life can change, and it is up to you to make decisions that will allow you to follow a new and different path. Personal enlightenment occurs when an ah-ha moment inspires you to follow a new path in life.

Be on the lookout for it. Don't settle for old patterns that could put you in decline. Look to the future with excitement and possibility and with a new interest that satisfies your curiosity. This is a beautiful moment when you can redirect your thinking, change your routines and daily patterns, and build an exciting new direction for your life. Wake up to its extraordinary possibilities.

You are in control of your thoughts, and you become what you believe.

—Darrin Donnelly

ASK: WHAT IS THE QUESTION?

To ask the 'right' question is far more important than to receive the answer. The solution of a problem lies in the understanding of the problem; the answer is not outside the problem, it is in the problem.

—Jiddu Krishnamurti

Life can be overwhelming at times with distractions, recurring problems, deadlines, caregiving, and conflicts. Taken all together, these problems can challenge our sanity or at the very least make our life extremely uncomfortable and worrisome. We might be constantly bombarded with issues needing to be resolved, illnesses needing a cure, and unfortunate social relationships needing repair. We are challenged with budgets and financial responsibilities. We are responsible for family needs, child guidance and caregiving. We seek personal, free time, but it doesn't seem to be available. So, we are constantly on the treadmill, confronting one anxiety after another. In our businesses, we face personnel issues, sales deficiencies, and the constant balancing of income and overhead. We are running pretty fast to keep up, and it seems like the race doesn't stop. It keeps going, and new issues are constantly entering the arena. Another problem to solve. Another challenge to fix.

Stop! It's time to get organized. Our ultimate goal in our personal and business life is to find happiness and joy in all of our activities and to get our life back into balance. When all these issues hit you at once, it is definitely time to take responsibility and start searching for answers. Let's see how we can resolve these issues and find a path to resolution. Consider the following process:

ISSUES AND RESOLUTIONS

1. Identify all the problems you are facing, the distractions that continue to get in your way and the issues that need resolution.
2. Write each of these problems down on a piece of paper or on your computer and separate them into the following categories: Personal, Professional, Family, Cultural, Health, Spiritual or Financial
3. Next to each of the problems write down the answer to this question: Why is it a problem?
4. After you have answered the previous questions, make out a new list and prioritize the problems in each category.
5. Review each problem and determine why it is important to your life to resolve the problem.
6. As you review the problems, determine which ones are having a detrimental effect on your life, values, and principles.

7. After you have analyzed the problems and compared the reasons why each one is a problem, select the three most important problems, the ones that really have a negative impact on your life and place them in priority order from one to three.

8. Start with problem one and make out a list of how you can confront the problem and find a resolution to the problem – solve it, fix it, change it, eliminate it, make it too small to be much of a problem, or accept it. Do this for each problem, one at a time, not all together, until you have found resolutions for all three. Then proceed to take action.

When you are finished resolving the first three, select the next three most important problems and run them through the same process.

The key to problem-solving is to minimize the impact of all the problems by simply taking one at a time. Choose the most important problem first, analyze the problem, see how it effects your life, determine how it effects your feelings, come to grips with the problem, and find a solution to the problem. Working with one at a time simplifies the process and eliminates the complexity of confronting all the problems you are facing at once. It is difficult to solve all your problems at one time, all together, but, taking one at a time simplifies the process and makes getting to a solution more accessible.

Now let's get to the more important question. Why are these problems and what is the question you are really trying to answer? Understanding the problem and refining the question are critical to being able to extract the most effective answer. When we don't understand the problem, our questions can be nebulous and off target. C.S. Lewis poses this question: "How many hours are there in a mile? Is yellow square or round? Probably half the questions we ask – half our great theological and metaphysical problems – are like that." I find his idea amusing as he emphasizes the confusion in the way we pose questions to ourselves.

Each problem you face is probably having a negative effect on your life and challenging your values, principles, and philosophy. This causes tension between your actions and your beliefs, and that begins to put you in a very uncomfortable position. Your life is not in harmony. Your life in not congruent, and there is a tremendous imbalance between your hopes and aspiration and your routines and actions. Originally, you may have thought that the question you were trying to answer had to do with a particular problem you were facing. But the process goes much deeper than that and will probably involve looking into your true desires, your aspirations for the future, and your desired feelings.

Your desired feelings drive all your decisions. That said, how do your problems hamper or conflict with your desired feelings? In the next chapter, we will take a closer look at how your feelings are a significant influence on your life and all the decisions you make. But for now, look at the three most important problems that need resolution. Let's say that one of the problems on your list is a conflict between you and one of your family members. It may be a philosophical incompatibility that always culminates in a heated discussion leaving you both in unpleasant moods. Looking at this situation, what is the problem? Obviously, the problem is the fact that you have two divergent philosophies which are creating a tension. You are not the problem, and the other family member is not the problem. It is a confrontation of two philosophies that will always conflict. However, a search for a common denominator could identify a better starting point for future discussions.

What is most important is asking yourself, "What am I trying to resolve?" As you begin to read the next chapter, I will ask you to list your most desired feelings. One of your feelings might be to live a life of peace and contentment in all your relationships. If that is a desired feeling in your life, it will help you connect the question with the problem you are trying to resolve. In the case of the family member and the incompatible philosophies, what you are really trying to solve is not how to change the family member, but how to maintain a life of peace and contentment. That is the question. That is the root cause of your feeling uncomfortable with the discussions with the family member. As you try to find a resolution, look first to the feeling you want to achieve.

Follow a sequence like this:

1. I want a life with peaceful relationships and contentment.
2. I will avoid situations that will interfere with a life of peace.
3. I will change or minimize relationships or discussions that instigate dissonance.
4. I will change or eliminate problems that cause anxiety.
5. I will plan a life that supports peace and contentment.

The real question is, "How can I create a life that reinforces my desire to experience peace and contentment in all of my actions and relationships?" Knowing that this is your real desire and the most important goal will help you understand the problems that are in conflict with your desired feelings. When you discover a problem, ask yourself why it is a problem and how it is affecting your feelings. Once you see this relationship, it becomes easier to determine the importance of the problem and to identify possible solutions.

Remember, there are some problems you can't solve. You may have to walk away from some problems, perhaps a person or a situation. You can't change someone else, at least not without tremendous effort. You may just have to walk away. But, most importantly, you must support your feelings and create a life that reinforces the way you want to feel. If your problems effect your feelings, you must find a way to change or eliminate the problem. You cannot live in conflict. But as you confront your problems, always go back to the two most important concerns: Why is it a problem and what is the question you are trying to answer?

There are no foolish questions and no man becomes a fool until he has stopped asking questions.

—Charles Proteus Steinmetz

UNLEASH YOUR DREAMS AND FANTASIES: TWELVE STEPS

1. Open your mind.
2. Unleash your imagination.
3. Encourage your curiosity.
4. Recognize your unfulfilled dreams and desires.
5. Identify your fantasies.
6. Approach life with optimism.
7. Identify new desired experiences.
8. Identify what is most important in your life.
9. List what you would like to accomplish personally.
10. List your professional aspirations.
11. Identify people who support your ambitions.
12. Visualize your ideal life.

UNLEASH YOUR DREAMS AND FANTASIES WORKSHEET

You have opened your mind, unleashed your imagination and begun to think about your life, your dreams, and your aspirations. To take action on these changes, make the following lists, never limiting yourself to the number of lines indicated.

List your most important unfulfilled dreams, desires and fantasies.

1._____

2._____

3._____

4._____

5._____

List what inspires your curiosity and what you would like to learn about.

1._____

2._____

3._____

4._____

5._____

List new experiences you would like to have.

1._____

2._____

3._____

4._____

5._____

List what you want to accomplish in your life, assuming you have no limits at all.

1._____

2._____

3._____

4._____

5._____

List the people who support, encourage, and reinforce your ambitions.

1._____

2._____

3._____

4._____

5._____

List your professional ambitions and aspirations.

1._____

2._____

3._____

4._____

5._____

List your personal ambitions and aspirations.

1._____

2._____

3._____

4._____

5._____

Of all the answers from the lists above, select the three most important that will help you manifest your ideal life. Write each as a goal-and-action statement. Example: I want to make an extended trip to France to study architecture, and in preparation I will do research and enroll in college level courses to study French architecture and culture.

1. I want to _____

   and in preparation I will _____

2. I want to _____

   and in preparation I will _____

3. I want to _____

   and in preparation I will _____

three

UNLEASH YOUR FEELINGS

RESPECT YOUR FEELINGS

I've learned that people will forget what you said, people will forget what you did, but people will never forget how you made them feel.

—Maya Angelou

EVERY DECISION WE MAKE is guided and influenced by our feelings. Rational judgment, research data and surveys are all important, but in the end, it is our feelings that finally prompt us to make a decision, any decision. How many years has a red convertible been on your wish list? How many times have you picked up a travel catalog and dreamed of taking a cruise down the Rhine or sailing the Mediterranean Sea? Are these based on rational judgments? Absolutely not. So, listen to your feelings. They are important. They are at the intersection of your subconscious and your conscious mind, and they will have more impact than you can imagine.

I have spent over forty years in marketing communications. In our communications with others, especially in this industry, we need to be keenly aware of the feelings of our clients and our client's customers. We need to listen carefully and clearly understand those with whom we communicate. We need to understand not only their beliefs, but why they believe in what they do and, most critically, how it makes them feel. What we can achieve by being aware of the feelings of those with whom we communicate is amazing. Why? Because although we are not conveying facts, we are communicating on an emotional level. We are speaking deeper than the surface. We are appealing to underlying desires, those that support feelings.

When you try to convince someone to see your way of thinking, do it by appealing to their feelings. Understand them. Speak to their feelings, and your communications will be much more successful.

Your feelings may not be backed up with evidence or critical data, but they are a significant part of your whole decision-making process. Brian Tracy said it perfectly: "Just as your car runs more smoothly and requires less energy to go faster and farther when the wheels are in perfect alignment, you perform better when your thoughts, feelings, emotions, goals, and values are in balance." Everything is in alignment, which is the basic principle of praxis or congruency.

As you make decisions for your life and plan your future, don't ignore your feelings. They are more important than your wish list. They drive your desires and set the mood for decision-making. Let your feelings prompt your imagination and guide you in making decisions for your future. The beginning phase of creativity is not the time for rational judgement. That comes much later. But this is the time for entering a dream state driven by your feelings and desires. Unleash your innermost feelings. Allow your imagination to flow and your creativity to surface with exciting new adventures for your future. If feelings govern your decision-making process, why not plan your future by making your feelings the goal?

Let's look at how we plan tasks and set priorities. We are all use "to-do" lists. I referred to this process briefly in a previous chapter. That usually involves listing all those things that you need to do that day or that week. That list might look something like this:

1. Take the car in for service.
2. Send thank-you card.
3. Organize file drawer.
4. Pay the weekly bills.
5. Shop for the birthday party.

These are mundane, but let's look more deeply at "to-do" lists. What if a "to-do" list was oriented toward achievement? If you proceeded with this in mind, your list might look something like this:

1. Register for a course on business finance.
2. Volunteer for a local charity where my talents can be used.
3. Plan a vacation to France to study Renaissance architecture.
4. Become a counselor at a summer camp for underprivileged children.
5. Take a leave of absence from work to get an MBA.
6. Spend a year at a monastery to study religion.

These two lists are very different! The first is insignificant compared to the second. This is what you could accomplish in life if, in addition to your first "to-do" list, you also created a list of desired achievements. These can be intermediate or long-term goals, but without them, you could be stuck in a rut of just doing that to-do list. To become significant, we have to get past the stuff that just needs to be done. We can look to the future and see our lives making major contributions and advancing to much higher levels.

Now, let's go one step further. Remember, feelings drive your decisions. So, what if you developed a new concept for lists and developed a list of feelings. How do you want to feel? We discussed this, briefly, in a previous chapter. What if you made a list of all the feelings you want as an end result of your accomplishment? For example, one feeling might be, "I want to feel intellectually stimulated." Or, "I want to feel like I have used my talents to help someone else." Or, "I want to feel spiritually at peace." This is just a start to the possibilities of how you may want to feel. Understanding your desired feelings will give you more impetus to detail your list of potential accomplishments.

Start with your feelings and map out a plan for achieving those feelings and then delineate your road map for accomplishing them. A feelings list might look something like this:

1. I want to feel at peace in all my relationships.
2. I want to feel a sense of accomplishment.
3. I want to feel healthy every day of my life.
4. I want to feel mentally sharp every day of my life.
5. I want to feel that I am growing intellectually.
6. I want to continue to feel compassion for those in need.

Now we have reasons for working on that accomplishment list. Now we have a "Why." And once we understand our purpose, our "How" is much easier to understand and accomplish. To make a connection with the three lists, let's start with the list of feelings. Select one feeling that you wish to have, then select one accomplishment that will help you make that feeling a reality. Then, select one activity that will help you get to that accomplishment.

1. I want to feel that I am growing intellectually (feelings list).
2. I want to pursue a college degree in environmental science (accomplishments list).
3. Research regional universities and apply for admission in a desired program (to-do list).

Let your feelings bring excitement and depth back into your life. Look back in time to find those events and relationships that influenced your feelings. Reflect on your youth and see yourself as a child, unencumbered by the demands of your current situation. How was it then? How did that make you feel? Do you remember the joys and enthusiasms of youth? How can we recapture the feelings of those days?

The point is not to throw out your ambition, but simply to be wary of allowing your ambition to control your fulfillment and believing that you have to be unhappy now in order to be happy someday. The reality is that there is no need to make yourself miserable pursuing a dream. Happiness is only found in the present moment.

—Emily Fletcher

FIND YOUR PASSION

There is nothing more turned on than a person with a dream and the guts to pick up the phone. Passion is the wind in your sails, and practicality is the rudder. You need both to get where you're going.

—Danielle LaPorte

Many life planning coaches say one's life must be in balance. They would have you believe that your commitment to your family, profession, finances, health, cultural achievements, spiritual needs, and personal ambitions must all be in balance. In fact, some have even developed a wheel of life chart that, if scored properly, would show an equal dedication to each of the important elements of your life, and hence bring about a well-balanced life. This is probably a good barometer to use if you want a well-balanced life. But first, ask yourself, "Why do I want a well-balanced life?" Every element of your life would be given equal attention and importance. It would be impossible to give 100% to any one category in your life. Consequently, you would go from one task to the other with a middle-of-the-road philosophy. So, decide what kind of life you desire.

A BALANCED LIFE

A life in equal balance assumes every area of your life is reasonably equal in importance and gives approximately equal attention to each.

A PASSION-DRIVEN LIFE

A life driven by passion assumes one, two or three areas of your life are more important and significantly increases the time and attention given to these.

To reach your full potential, your actions must be driven by passion. In *The Fire Starter Sessions,* Danielle LaPorte describes the desirability of a balanced life as a myth.

Passion will put your life into the right proportions that work as a whole…When passion is a priority – passion for family, for vocation, for meaning – your energy intensifies. And when your energy is more focused, more aimed, you begin to care less about the things that don't really matter.

Passion implies a full dedication, an overwhelming desire for what must be achieved, satisfied, or accomplished. Great scientists, writers, musicians, inventors, and so many other professionals approach their life with a passion and dedication to an idea – a problem that must be solved, a story that must be written, a musical score that must find its way to the musical staff and an invention that must be introduced to the world. This is passion. It wakes you up in the middle of the night. It is on your mind throughout the day, and it guides your decision to act. When passion takes over your life, you become driven to achieve and to satisfy its calling.

Walt Disney had a passion. He had a vision of something that did not exist. He wanted to build a place where you could temporarily leave your current reality and enter a world of fantasy, yesterday and tomorrow. What a vision! What a passion! And he accomplished his passion in Disneyland. His passion continues in an ever-changing, ever-growing vision. A dream. A passion. A reality. So many writers have said that we need to have a vision of our future. But we also need to understand exactly where we are now—our current reality. From this present reality we can begin to develop a roadmap for where we intend to go. Disney had that vision and was able to develop a roadmap for how he would get there. Esther and Jerry Hicks say, in *Ask and It is Given,* "An understanding of both where you are and where you want to be is essential if you are to make any deliberate decision about your journey."

Throughout this book I have highlighted many ideas that will help you begin to plan your vision, but one of the most important ones is passion. You may have a desire. You may have a dream or a wish. But it is your decision to work toward these dreams that makes a dream a passion, one that will get you moving and start you on your road to change. How can you find the passion that is important enough to guide your life changes? Simon Sinek suggests considering the phrase "Just Cause." Your passion is intertwined with your beliefs, values, principles and all the things that you cherish and feel are important. Perhaps it is a cause that already exists or one that you can originate. Perhaps it is centered around improvement in education or advancements in the arts and culture or finding a cure for a devastating disease. Maybe it is an idea that needs to be communicated. Using himself as an example, Sinek says,

> My Just Cause is to build a world in which the vast majority of people wake up inspired, feel safe at work and return home fulfilled at the end of the day, and I am looking for as many people as possible who will join me in this Cause.

As I reflect on Sinek's 'Just Cause,' I am inspired by his dedication and concern for his fellow man, his generosity, and his desire to have as many people as possible join his cause and spread his philosophy.

Throughout this book, I have asked you to allow your dreams and desires to surface and to use your imagination as you look at your life and make changes for the future. Now, I encourage you to find your true passion. What is exceedingly important to you? It may be found in your profession, your hobbies, your family, or your religion. It may be a specific cause or charity that you would like to dedicate your life to supporting. Or it might be a philosophy that you want to convert into a book that you feel would be a wonderful influence on children as they approach various stages of their lives. What really excites you? What are you good at? What do you really love to do? What can be selected from all of your life experiences that you have always wished you could pursue. How can you dedicate your life to achievements that will allow you to leave a dynamic legacy?

If we are to make a significant contribution to the creation of peace and healing in the world, we cannot remain enmeshed in the smallness of our family story. We must allow our story to become larger—we must take our place in the rich expanse of our true nature, in deep kinship with all creation.

—Wayne Muller

EMBRACE OPTIMISM

When I talk about a positive reality, I'm not talking about one in which good things magically happen by the sheer power of positive thinking; I'm talking about one in which you can summon all your cognitive, intellectual, and emotional resources to create positive change, because you believe that true change is possible.

—Shawn Achor

One of the most inspiring books I read recently is *Before Happiness,* written by Shawn Achor. A leader in the positive psychology movement, Achor teaches us about the importance and perhaps even the necessity of having a positive and optimistic attitude while approaching all aspects of our life. If you are the designer of your life, then what mindset would work to your advantage as you approach your new life design? You get to choose your reality both now and in the future. A person who chooses optimism in their life will be rewarded in two ways: first, they will have a much more successful outcome to their mission, and second, they will have much more happiness and joy during the process.

When you embark on a task with a positive attitude, you can see the future more clearly, create a more exciting vision of the outcome and have much more confidence in your pursuit. And let's remember, we are not just looking to solve a problem as we look to our future, we are trying to reshape our future to be filled with excitement, thrilling opportunities and wonderful new adventures. So, give yourself a fighting chance for success. As Covey would say, "Start with the end in mind." And if I can take the liberty of combining Achor and Covey's words, for a greater chance of success, start optimistically with the end in mind.

Optimism is essential to letting the imagination run wild. You must be confident that anything you dream, any desire begging to surface could be successful. Optimism allows you to proceed with confidence, experimenting and expecting that your efforts will not be wasted but will meet with success. Open the door to a vast array of possibilities. Optimism will allow you to choose freely and know that when the choice is made, there are real possibilities that your dreams will be achieved.

To the artist, the blank canvas is filled with possibilities and excitement. To the architect and designer, the blank sheet of paper or computer screen is screaming with potential. What could be? What dreams could be realized? What exciting new experiences can be created with an unrestricted palette of possibilities? To the musician, the musical score is waiting to be diagrammed with the magical notes that create the soothing melodies of a ballad or the exciting movements of a symphonic rhapsody with full orchestration. To the scientist who experiments and searches for answers to a critical problem the answer is waiting, somewhere, and will be found. These are all creative challenges supported by the belief that success is possible. At the onset of this type of creative challenge, we must approach it with optimism, knowing that in the end, a masterpiece may surface, experimentation may yield amazing results, and confidence will guide every stage of expression.

Life if much more exciting if we can approach it with an optimistic spirit. I cannot imagine going through life with anything but an optimistic spirit. With optimism, the decisions we make will reward us with the fulfillment of our dreams, and every road we walk will culminate in finding the answers to our search. Optimism must be the first step in any creative act, in any imaginative search and in any innovative pursuit.

Many experts claim that if we focus on the negatives, we will get more of the same—negative responses, negative answers, and negative results. If we focus on all the reasons why we shouldn't or can't, the results will be the same—we won't and we can't. You get what you think about all the time, so it is vital to set your mind to thinking optimistically, knowing that you can succeed. Darrin Donnelly, in his book *Relentless Optimism,* says,

> Success begins in your mind. But failure does too. Optimism is self-fulfilling, but so is pessimism. You have to decide how you're going to think. The choice is yours, and you have to own the outcome.

BE MOTIVATED, BE CONFIDENT

Ability is what you're capable of doing. Motivation determines what you do. Attitude determines how well you do it.

—Lou Holtz

Every successful venture begins with motivation. I taught thousands of students at the University of Illinois and the University of Akron over thirty years, and I believed that motivating students right at the start was essential for creating an atmosphere of confidence and respect, both for my students and for myself as the teacher. What I found to be most important was to first instill self-confidence – my students' belief in themselves, in their chosen field and in their dedication to their profession. Second, I needed to give my students good reason to believe that I was able to help them gain the knowledge and skills to help them advance in their field of study. I began this by complimenting my students for choosing their field of study and expressing the importance of their contribution to their profession. I had to inspire them and help them understand that working in their chosen profession would be a thrilling experience with new adventures around every corner. Their challenge was to remain focused on their future vision, allow their hopes and dreams to surface and avoid the distractions that constantly impede their progress.

In my marketing communications firm, I worked with hundreds of CEOs and business leaders around the world and found that effective communication begins with motivation there as well. These business leaders needed to know that I respected them, their businesses and their products and services. They needed to understand that I believed in what they were doing and how their products or services benefitted their customers. I needed to compliment them right up front and express my excitement about working with their company. I had to inspire confidence and convince them that my company was the best choice for helping them reach their marketing goals.

One of the most important words in personal improvement is motivation; it is the key to kick-starting new directions in life. Without the right attitude, you can become stuck in the routine of everyday activities. These distractions get in the way of making a difference. Motivation is inspiring; it is the underlying engine that creates the propulsion to help you take the most important first step in launching a new business, a new career or a new project that has been waiting in the wings.

Motivation provides the stimulus for success in business or life. It is the most important first step in any communication where results are expected. Motivation is especially important in working with a member of your staff or project team. As a leader, you need to motivate people to believe in themselves and let them know you are there to help them accomplish the task at hand. Successful communications might follow the steps listed below:

1. Be excited and enthusiastic in your communication.
2. Motivate the person with whom you are communicating.
3. Give compliments and praise to the person.
4. Instill confidence in the person's abilities.
5. Explain why they are the right person for the task at hand.
6. Express the importance of the task and define its purpose.
7. Provide instructions on how to accomplish the task.
8. Assign the task with assurance that you are available to help along the way.

Everyone needs to know why. We all ask, why am I doing this task? How will this help our company, our client or me personally? How does this fit into the overall plan? If you follow the steps listed above, most of these questions will be answered. We all want to know that we are important and that we are working for an important purpose. Providing answers to these questions helps to advance the motivational process. In teaching and in business, I've learned that you can't accomplish anything until you motivate first. Whether it's motivating an employee, a family member, a student or even yourself, motivation must come first. Once you have provided this critical inspiration, it becomes much easier to teach, lead or assign a task.

Everyone has a dream. Unfortunately, going through our daily work and mindless routines, that dream can become tarnished. The original excitement of envisioning the dream can be lost in the responsibilities of life. But the dream can still live in our subconscious and needs to be revived and brought to the surface. It needs to be brought back into our current reality, and we need to be inspired by the exciting new life embodied in that dream. There is a process for inspiring and motivating people to accomplish their dreams and live the life that they have imagined. But first they need to be motivated. For a business leader, manager, teacher, or anyone in a position of leadership, the motivational process could follow this progression:

1. Compliment an employee or student on their choice of profession.
2. Express how important they are to the world by having chosen to do this work.
3. Let them know how important their commitment is.
4. Reinforce their need for knowledge and understanding in their field of study.
5. Get them excited about the importance of providing something the world needs.

6. Encourage them to visualize themselves in the future as successful professionals.
7. Inspire them to make a difference and to make a significant contribution to their business, their community and society.

First, we compliment, then inspire, then encourage, then show them their potential and point the way to reaching it. This is the motivational process. After this motivational introduction, you can begin to teach, assign tasks, and open a discussion. Guide them. Inspire them. Give them confidence.

This book shows you how to create an exceptional life, a life that follows your dreams to create an exciting future. This is not the typical life planning book. Only a small part of it talks about setting goals, prioritizing, and scheduling. It goes much deeper into motivation, inspiration, and confidence, concentrating on unleashing your dreams and imagination. Until you know what you want and why you want it, why bother setting goals and schedules? Let's find out who you are and unwrap all those dreams hidden within. Then, you will have the possibility of creating the life that you want and desire.

We need to be motivated to approach this process with excitement and enthusiasm. Set the stage for this new experience. Believe in yourself. And get ready to open your mind to discovery.

Desire is the key to motivation, but it's determination and commitment to an unrelenting pursuit of your goal—a commitment to excellence—that will enable you to attain the success you see.

—Mario Andretti

SEE IN PERSPECTIVE

You cannot see what you don't look for, and you cannot look for what you don't believe in.

—Darren Hardy

The Renaissance opened the eyes of painters to one of the most magnificent phenomena – the ability to represent the world in three dimensions. As the laws of perspective were discovered, they influenced the world of art, architecture, design, and all the visual arts. Painting could now portray the way we really see, and architectural designs and illustrations could be drawn with the use of vanishing points, receding planes and realistic spatial relationships. As a professor of art, I enjoyed teaching the laws of perspective drawing to students in art, design, and architecture. Perspective drawing can involve many processes and several techniques. These are the basic elements of a perspective drawing:

1. The object to be drawn.
2. A place where the viewer is standing and viewing the object (the station point).
3. The picture plane (the transparent plane placed between the object and the viewer on which the drawing is envisioned).
4. Lines of sight that move from the eyes of the viewer to points on the object. These lines of sight intersect the picture plane.
5. Finally, the drawing is created on the picture plane (the paper) guided by the intersecting lines of sight.

The intersecting points on the picture plane indicate where the object is drawn. This appears to be fairly simple, but in practice can be quite complex. But let's simplify the process for now. To create a true perspective drawing, place a piece of glass between you and the object. See the object through the glass. Draw the object that you see on the piece of glass. Be sure not to move your head or your eyes while you draw. Where you stand, relative to the object being drawn, will determine how the object will look. If you were to move a little to the left or right or up or down, the drawing of the object would change. That is called your point of view. This process of seeing an object in perspective is like using a camera to photograph an object or scene. We stand still at a station point, view the object through the view finder and transfer the image on the flat surface of the film or flat digital memory card. The image is then presented on a flat computer screen or printed on a flat sheet of paper. This is the same concept used in the drawing process. The results are the same, translating a three-dimensional scene onto a two-dimensional plane.

Now let's get into how the idea of perspective affects us, not in an artist's or architect's drawing, but as human beings. What is your point of view? That's what is so important in the way you see things, hear things, and perceive reality. Where do you stand on various issues, and how do you form your opinions? Usually, they are dependent on your point of view. As in perspective drawing, you stand at a selected station point and see various objects in front of you. You know that what you see will be different from each new angle. Some might say that the key is to place yourself in the best point of view for your desired outcome. However, your selection of a point of view will also influence your approach to seeing, and your perceptions will be guided by that point of view. I encourage you to be flexible in selecting your point of view so you can see things from many points of view. This will open your mind to be able to see additional and alternative possibilities.

I recently participated in a webinar facilitated by Rebecca Ryan. Ms. Ryan, a futurist who founded Next Generation Consulting, helps clients re-evaluate their current reality and shape their future based on their new vision. The webinar topic, "Causal Layered Analysis" (CLA), dealt with the concept of looking at problems and seeing them on many different levels. Often, we see a problem and perceive it on a surface level, only seeing the problem and its effects. But Ryan challenged us to see deeper into the problem, to understand the causes of the problem and the systems and influences that perpetuate the problem. We cannot make quick assumptions without understanding underlying causes. We too need to look deeply into our life and understand the causes that motivate us and direct us to make the kinds of decisions that we do. According to Ryan, "If we want better futures, we need better stories." She claims that if we create a new story for our lives, we will live into that story. Many other writers advocate variations of this idea:

- "You will attract what you think about."
- "Become the author of your life."
- "To change something, build a new model so good that it makes the old model obsolete."

What we envision (our story) will motivate us to attract the elements of our new life (our preferred future). Rebecca Ryan is one of those motivational personalities who really brings about change. Her commitment to future generations is inspiring, and her seminars, workshops and consulting practice help people, business leaders and government officials think about their future and planning processes with more creativity. Does that sound familiar? We need to do that same thing for our lives. We need to write our own story for our future and allow it to unfold as we move toward executing our goals.

When you look at an object, a situation, or a problem, you need to know where you are standing relative to that object or problem. Remember, your point of view will change your perception of the problem or the object that you are viewing. Knowing that, it is to your advantage to be aware of your position as you view a problem, an opportunity or a situation. Where you stand governs the way you approach solving the problem. So, before you dive into finding a solution for a problem, make sure that you first understand these things:

1. Where you have chosen to stand in relation to the problem (your point of view).
2. What the problem really is.
3. Why it is a problem.
4. Why the problem exists.
5. How the problem affects your life.

You must be absolutely truthful in each case to generate the most accurate results. Assumptions made in selecting your point of view, right from the beginning, will jade the results of your research or problem-solving process. You see what you think about. You see what you expect to see. And if you understand this, your approach to solving the problem will be more transparent.

Next, don't get stuck on just one point of view. To understand people, we need to put ourselves in their place—understand their point of view and see things from their station point. Because where you are standing will change the look of the object that you see. We have the capacity to change our point of view and therefore see things from a different vantage point. But, throughout the process, know that you are seeing from a particular point of view. Changing your point of view can help unleash your imagination, get a true understanding of the problem, including why it is a problem for you.

The previous paragraphs explain how we see in perspective and what choices we have in selecting a point of view. But even if you are not interested in becoming an artist, you are interested in understanding how you see and what that means. We know that positioning ourselves relative to an object will give us a specific view. But, knowing why we see what we see is perhaps the most important factor and has altogether to do with our point of view. As we approach resolving a problem or making a change in our life, we come to it with certain pre-judgements. These influence what we see and why we see. We enter into the realm of visual perceptions when we ask ourselves these questions,

- Why do we see what we see?
- Are we really seeing what we see?
- Is our vision clouded by our prejudices?

As we look at a problem, consider the results we want from resolving the problem and why they matter. We often approach our research with preconceptions. These preconceptions will influence our point of view and what results we might be expecting. So, clearly understand where you are coming from when you approach your research and try to see the problem from as many points of view as possible so that you can afford yourself as many options as possible for resolutions. Then you can choose the best approach to resolving the problem. To be able to discover the most accurate answers, seeing the real truth is essential.

The last approach to seeing in perspective is to see the total picture. Often, we get caught up in the details. We are too close to the problem. We need to stand back, change our station point, see the entire object before us, so that we can perceive the entire image, the entire problem, and its impact on us. Seeing details will only indicate part of the problem, but seeing the problem as a whole and how it relates to all the other parts will give you a better probability for a more effective and realistic solution. Stand back. Move around a little. See the problem from different points of view in order to select the most advantageous and most appropriate perspective. Give yourself the best opportunity for success.

As I explain this visual approach to seeing in perspective, I refer to the object or problem. But our concern may not be to solve a problem or view an object. It may be to discover new opportunities. It may be to understand another person's reasoning. It might be a search to solve a relationship problem. Or, more importantly, it might be to envision a new future. In this book I am talking about change—change in your future and in your life. Change must come from a real confrontation with the issues, unclouded by pre-judgements. As you approach changes to your current reality or your preferred future, try selecting several points of view to expand your horizon and unearth many additional opportunities.

Designers know that you never go with your first idea. Designers know that when you choose from lots of options you choose better.

—Bill Burnett and Dave Evans

UNDERSTAND PERCEPTION

Creating more positive perceptions of our goals can dramatically increase our engagement, focus, productivity, and motivation and thus increase the speed at which we attain them.

—Shawn Achor

What do we see? What do we hear? What do we believe? These are all governed by our perceptions of reality. What is reality? It all depends on your perception—at least for you. Having worked in the visual arts for most of my life, let me share a story that could further explain the meaning of the word, "perception." Imagine five people attending an art opening at a museum displaying abstract paintings. Let's select just one painting for this example. First, we know that even though there are many people viewing the painting, the painting remains the same. It doesn't change. The painting is comprised of color, lines, and shapes in a composition, and the painting is defined by the way these elements are integrated. Yet, when five observers view the painting, they may all have different perceptions of what it is saying or the message the artist tried to convey.

As an abstract painter, I have had paintings exhibited in one-person and group shows from New York City to Los Angeles. It is always interesting to talk with visitors, hear their questions and listen to their observations about my paintings. Many respond by seeing something in the painting, like dancers, animals, or ocean waves. Many say that they see dramatic movement in the painting, and that the movement expresses a certain feeling. Many respond to color saying that, "My favorite color is blue, and I love the blue in this painting." All approach it from a different point of view. All will have a particular reason for responding the way they do.

In other words, each has a different perception of the painting. My grandson, upon viewing one of my paintings said, "Grandpa, it's obvious, there is a chipmunk right there in the painting." We all see things, hear things, and react to situations based on our history, our developed preferences, and our education. And all this forms how we see and hear things – our perceptions.

"When the student is ready the teacher will appear." This famous quotation embodies the essence of perception. We see what we have been influenced to see. We see what we are ready to see. We see what we want to see. We don't see what we don't want to see. We are jaded by our experiences and prejudices, whatever those might be. Therefore, if we realize that our perceptions are influenced by our past experiences and we take the time to analyze how those experiences form our perceptions, we can change our thinking and how we perceive things.

According to psychologist Richard Gregory,

> Our perceptions of the world are hypotheses based on past experiences and stored information. Sensory receptors receive information from the environment, which is then combined with previously stored information about the world which we have built up as a result of experience. The formation of an incorrect hypothesis will lead to errors of perception.

We control our lives, but our past experiences influence our thinking and perception. Therefore, we need to approach our judgments with clear and rational thinking, understanding that we arrive at all situations with a prejudiced viewpoint. We have pre- judged the painting, the report, or the people we are about to meet, and our perceptions control our initial impressions and color our full understanding.

We make the decisions that affect our future. What kind of future do you want? A clearly defined vision of your future is necessary for you to establish the building blocks for getting there. To paraphrase Thoreau, build your castles in the sky and then construct the foundations for them. See the vision first and then determine how to get there. But our perceptions will need to be altered. Do we see things from a positive or negative point of view? Do we see things as good or bad? If you want to change your future and achieve your new vision for your life, you need to change your perceptions and make adjustments that corelate with your new goals and ambitions. You can find the good or bad in everything and everyone you encounter. Which do you prefer? It's all a matter of your understanding and adjusting your perceptions. According to Wayne Dyer, "When you change the way you look at things, the things you look at change." The things are the same and have always been the same, but your perception can change to make them different.

You have the ability to make a rational judgment about how you perceive things. Understand who you are. Understand your beliefs. Design your new future and determine what it will take to change your perceptions so that all your encounters will reinforce your ability to achieve your vision for your future.

Your perception is your reality.

—Bob Proctor

EXPECT THE BEST

Today, expect something good to happen to you no matter what occurred yesterday. Realize the past no longer holds you captive. It can only continue to hurt you if you hold on to it. Let the past go. A simply abundant world awaits.

—Sarah Breathnach

Are you living with an expectant attitude? If not, why not? Expectation is directly related to confidence. If you feel confident that something will happen or that you can accomplish something, it has a much better chance of actually coming to pass. Expectation is also related to optimism. Optimism inspires confidence, and confidence gives you the belief that you can accomplish anything that you have set out to do.

Expecting that you will accomplish your goals or dreams also encourages you to make sure that you do everything possible to make those goals become a reality. You cannot fail at achieving your mission, and if some early attempts do, you will continue trying until it is accomplished. After all, you expect it to happen. You expect it to become a reality. There is no second guessing. It will happen.

Everything you do should be done with an expectant attitude. Questioning a goal only gets in the way of your achieving it. If your goals and desires are well thought through and properly researched, you will be able to achieve them and expecting them to happen reinforces your actions to make sure that they do happen.

Expect success in everything you do. Expect joy in your life. Expect happiness along the way, and approach all of life with an expectant, optimistic attitude. Why not? If you fail, you will try again and eventually achieve your mission. It is well established that patients who go into surgery with a positive, optimistic, and confident attitude have a much higher rate of success than those who do not. Your subconscious works with you and for you and lends additional support to the process.

In the *Art of Living*, Bob Proctor puts it this way,

> If you can see it, then you can do it. How are you going to do it? Well, you'll be able to tell the person that after you do it. It's not all locked up in your intellect. It's locked up in faith. It's locked up in the belief that if you hold the idea in your mind, you'll move into the vibration that will attract it.... You become what you are thinking about.

Expecting a positive outcome is not fantasy. It is the reinforcement that we all need to keep going, keep trying, and keep experimenting until we reach success. After all, we can't disappoint ourselves – we expect it to happen.

SAVOR ANTICIPATION

Never forget that anticipation is an important part of life. Work's important, family's important, but without excitement, you have nothing. You're cheating yourself if you refuse to enjoy what's coming.

—Nicholas Sparks

What generates the excitement of an event, a vacation, or a party? It's the anticipation of getting there, being there, doing something or participating in an event. Looking forward to something fills every day with promise. Remember, happiness is not the result, it is the way. And anticipating a future occurrence is a sure way of bringing about happiness and excitement every day. That is what is important about planning for the future. It is the anticipation of the plan being fulfilled. Looking forward to seeing that college friend, enjoying a concert, or purchasing a new home all adds to the thrill of living – anticipating that special occasion.

Anticipation is all about feelings of excitement, feelings of happiness, feelings of expecting a thrilling experience. "I can't wait" is an expression you say or hear while you are anticipating a future event or meeting. We need to plan special activities, events, and experiences in our lives because of how it makes us feel today, getting ready for that experience and anticipating the joy you will feel when the day finally arrives. Anticipation can be the actualization of the dream you envision and the fulfillment of your imagination. It can materialize your hope for the future or realize a long-awaited desire.

How do you want to feel? Remember, your feelings are what it is all about. Feelings guide your decisions, and the decisions you make define the degree of joy in your life. But don't wait until your decisions are realized. Become excited about your intentions along the way and anticipate the joy and excitement that you expect to experience. A well-planned vacation can last many months, even if it's only a week long, by anticipating all of the places that you plan to visit and activities you intend to participate in. Give yourself permission to think like this:

"I'm looking forward to that trip to the ocean."
"I can't wait for the wedding."
"I'm so excited to visit that historic museum in New York City."
"It's only two months until I move into my new home."

All along the way we are anticipating the realization of our dreams. And all the time leading up to that special event we are thrilled, excited, and eager to see our dreams come true. Be excited about life. Look forward to the weeks, months, and years ahead. Think optimistically and be thrilled about the new experiences you are going to have. The future looks bright as you enthusiastically anticipate the end results of your positive planning. Anticipating is an important part of your life. Unleash it, and feel the excitement it will bring to your life every day.

That sanguine expectation of happiness which is happiness itself.

—Jane Austen

FOLLOW YOUR INSPIRATION

When you are inspired by some great purpose, some extraordinary project, all your thoughts break their bonds; Your mind transcends limitations, your consciousness expands..., and you find yourself in a new, great and wonderful world. Dormant forces, faculties and talents become alive, and you discover yourself to be a greater person by far than you ever dreamed yourself to be.

—Patanjali

As we form our beliefs and principles in life, we look back to people and experiences that have been an influence and inspiration. Religious leaders, coaches, authors, teachers, friends, family members, and others may have been some of those who have made an impact on our thinking. Each of these individuals or experiences have provided an inspiration that helped to direct our thinking and establish our values, beliefs and principles. It is good to recall experiences we have had that helped shape our knowledge and belief system. These experiences will be diverse and touch on a variety of aspects of our beliefs and values.

For example, in 1972, I attended the Aspen Design Conference in Colorado. This was an exceptional event with prominent architects, designers, civic leaders, and scientists participating as speakers and guests. I chose to attend a workshop with Milton Glaser of New York City, one of the country's leading graphic designers, and responsible for the phase "I Love New York," with the heart replacing the word "Love." This classic design is still used today to promote travel to New York. It was exciting to be in a workshop with Glaser since I had referred to his work many times in my teaching. During the session, we were given an assignment to work on a project, the intent of which was to learn more about ourselves. Through this self-analysis, we were directed to a better understanding of our beliefs, our values, our responsibilities to our profession and to other people in our lives. In the discovery process, students chose a variety of methods including mid-mapping, list-making, writing stories and a variety of graphic solutions that exemplified their life story. At the end of the sessions, we all shared our experience in creating our personal solutions to the exercise. During this process I made an insightful discovery about myself, who I am and how I related to the people in my life. I concluded that, "I am responsible for my life, I am in control of my life and, most importantly, I am the designer of my life." Nearly fifty years after this workshop, I remember the experience vividly as a turning point in my life.

A second turning-point experience occurred at the University of Akron, where I was a professor in the School of Art, teaching courses in graphic design. We invited Buckminster Fuller, the internationally recognized architect and inventor of the geodesic dome, to speak to design students and faculty. Mr. Fuller sat in a comfortable chair in the corner of the room surrounded by several dozen students and faculty. He spoke extemporaneously for over two hours about architecture, design, and his personal philosophy. Fuller's presentation incorporated many of his ideas and perceptions about the future, but he primarily talked about the changes our world needs for civilization to survive. This idea is what I remember most and have continued to be inspired by. He said, "You never change things by fighting the existing reality. To change something, build a new model that makes the existing model obsolete."

In other words, you are the designer of your life. Take control of your life. Take control of your situation, whatever it might be. Design or develop a new life that is so much better, so much more exciting, it makes your current life obsolete and undesirable. To me, this is a concept I have tried to live by. Do not complain about your current reality, change it by creating a new model. This is under your control. You can make these decisions. You are responsible to make these decisions and create an extraordinary life. As Ralph Waldo Emerson said, "The only person you are destined to become is the person you decide to be."

Another inspiration to me was Frank Lloyd Wright. As a person born in Chicago and a student of architecture, Frank Lloyd Wright was someone who I admired from my early days in college for his philosophy and for his exceptional ability to design beautiful buildings and architectural details. I have visited many of his buildings and on dozens of occasions have visited and attended lectures at his Taliesin West campus in Scottsdale, Arizona. Wright's designs instilled in me a high respect for aesthetics and unparalleled design detailing. Wright inspired me to respect beauty in all forms. In his words, "The longer I live, the more beautiful life becomes. If you foolishly ignore beauty, you will soon find yourself without it. But if you invest in beauty, it will remain with you all the days of your life."

Wright's entire focus was on his commitment to architecture, his search for beauty and his respect for music and theater. All of the arts guided his activities in life. On a few occasions, I had the opportunity to meet with one of Wright's students, Vernon Swaback, who studied with Wright at Taliesin, founded Swaback Partners, in Scottsdale, Arizona and has written many books on architectural design, designing with nature and the future of our communities. He understands the commitment professionals must make to be successful in their practice. He recalls his experience as Wright's student: "During my time at Taliesin, there was no such thing as 'after work,' nor any notion of there being an 'after school.'" In other words, your passion is your life. There is no down time. Your involvement is twenty-four hours a day, seven days a week. What a tremendous inspiration, to be so involved that your work is a constant part of your life. Do you have that level of commitment to your work, your passion, and your profession? If not, why not? It is your life.

You are in control. You have the right to make decisions in your life that create the roadmap for your future.

An author for whom I have tremendous respect is Thich Nhat Hahn, a Buddhist monk who has written many books about his experiences in life, his time spent at the monastery and his memories of the horrors of the Vietnam War. In his spiritual teachings, Hahn tells us of his respect for life and for the present moment – the now. He also talks about the process of awakening our deepest desires. He says,

> Everyone has a dream. You need to take the time to be still, to look deeply, and to listen to your heart to find out what your deepest desire is. …Our dream gives us vitality. It gives our life meaning…. Living each moment as a way to realize our dreams, there is no difference between the end and the means.

What an inspiration he is! His respect for the Now, the current moment, is inspiring. He sees that we have a chance to cherish each day, each hour, each minute. He reminds us that the Now is all that we have and that we must respect each detail, each minute of our lives.

Another inspiration is Thomas Moore, whom I met recently at the Unicorn Writers Conference, in White Plains, New York. He was one of the leading speakers at the conference. Moore has written books on topics relating to the soul and the aging process. His book, *Care of the Soul,* is his flagship work.

In *Ageless Soul,* Moore talks about retirement and the anxieties those who are facing retirement can experience. His thoughts might be summarized in this one very simple sentence, "I like to think of retirement as a time to re-tire." What a simple concept, but absolutely on target. Retirement, at whatever age you choose, is a time to put on new tires, tune up your engine and create a new roadmap for life. Retirement might arrive at an early age or not until your 70s or 80s. Whatever your age, it is a time of change and a time to build a new model as Fuller puts it, or a time to replace the old tires with new ones, as Moore says. This is an exciting time in life. I see it as the enlightenment phase, when we can begin again and make a fresh start. But understand – any time is the right time to begin again and make a fresh start. You don't have to be at an obvious turning point. When you realize you are stuck in your life and constrained by your daily routine, start dreaming. Start opening your mind and becoming curious about your possibilities. Start creating and building new adventures that can take you to a more exciting and meaningful life.

Who are your mentors? Who has been an inspiration for you along the way? Look back over your life and highlight those who have had an impact, those who have presented you with powerful ideas that have lasted throughout your life and those who have been an inspiration. They are all part of you.

Openness to experience typically precedes inspiration, ... suggesting that those who are more open to inspiration are simply more likely to experience it.

—Scott Barry Kaufman

UNBRIDLE YOUR ENTHUSIASM

If you don't love what you're doing with unbridled passion and enthusiasm, you're not going to succeed when you hit obstacles.

—Howard Schultz

As you discovered in a previous section, your feelings are the most important influence for the actions you take in your life. If you feel optimistic, you can accomplish almost anything and reach any goal you set. If you feel hesitant, most projects will not get finished and will remain in a holding pattern until you see an encouraging sign. If you feel fearful or nervous about something that you are considering doing, you may not even get started. Your feelings will give you the go-ahead or stop you dead in your tracks.

But what if you approached life with enthusiasm, an even higher step than optimism? Better yet, what if you approached life with unbridled enthusiasm? Imagine a child rushing to experience her first

Christmas morning with lights glowing, presents everywhere, the scent of fresh-baked cookies? Can you picture a young sailor purchasing his first boat and imagining the thrill of his first launching and the excitement of crashing through the waves? Can you envision the last inning of the last game of the World Series where the score is tied, the fans are screaming, the tension is immense, and you are at bat, the pitch is thrown, and you hit a home run to win the game and the entire World Series? These are moments of unbridled enthusiasm—a level of excitement unparalleled by previous events, special enough to make you jump for joy. Such moments capture all your dreams, desires, and ambitions at one time and in one single vision.

Why not go through life this way? Why not design your life, your ambitions, and your activities in such an interesting and exciting way that your life is driven by unbridled enthusiasm? This must be the ultimate in optimistic thinking. Of course, we need optimism to even approach enthusiasm. And we must be enthusiastic to be able to reach its highest level – unbridled enthusiasm. Can you imagine the possibilities when you release your imagination, explore your hopes and dreams, and visualize your desires and aspirations with this level of enthusiasm?

Free exploration becomes much more doable when you are confident of the process. Open-minded curiosity is filled with possibilities if we can approach our research with the expectation of successful results. But, if we begin any endeavor with enthusiasm born of optimism and confidence, we can be assured of more successful results, and most importantly, an exciting process along the way. Happiness is the way. An exciting life is the way. Living an extraordinary life is the way. Living with unbridled enthusiasm makes the way an exceptional experience.

In a previous section I referred to the process of visual selection. What will you allow yourself to see? How will what you see influence your thinking, your feelings, and your attitude? Imagine going online and searching for a store that sold glasses – the kind that improve your vision – what if you could not only improve your vision, but also change the way you see things? What if you could buy glasses that gave you this kind of new vision?

1. Glasses to see with optimism
2. Glasses to enhance your curiosity
3. Glasses to open your mind
4. Glasses to reinforce your positive thinking
5. Glasses to see beauty
6. Glasses to open your eyes to new possibilities, new horizons and ambitions
7. Glasses to see everything with enthusiasm

Which glasses would you purchase? Imagine seeing through such glasses. With them, you could choose what and how you were seeing. With them, you could open your mind to a world of optimism, of beauty or excitement. Think of all the new experiences you could have, the new adventures and new projects you could undertake knowing that they could be completed with success. Such glasses may cost a little extra, but I would choose the glasses that let me see with unbridled enthusiasm. To those who say wearing rose-colored glasses is pollyannaish, I say, no. By seeing a world of beauty and hope, we live more happily and accomplish more. How can this be wrong?

What selection would you make to define your way of living? Would you approach life with enthusiasm – unbridled enthusiasm? Remember, you attract what you are thinking about. You are more likely to achieve what you select as a desired future.

All we need to make us really happy is something to be enthusiastic about.
—Charles Kingsley

SELECT THE EXCEPTIONAL

When a person starts to talk about their dreams, it's as if something bubbles up from within. Their eyes brighten, their face glows, and you can feel the excitement in their words.

—John C. Maxwell

Perhaps the most important chapter title in this book is this one. Your feelings govern your experiences. Approaching each day with a positive attitude will bring about better results. In the end, what we should attempt to attract into our lives is enhanced excitement – about the day, the activity, and the present moment. Everyone deserves an exciting life of thrilling experiences, fulfilled desires and pleasurable moments.

What do you have to do to reach exceptional levels of excitement? First, it is essential to design activities and events to stretch your imagination, dreams that become so powerful that anticipation provides a level of excitement far beyond the norm. Don't be satisfied with the status quo, the regular routines. Select the exceptional and be committed to making it happen. With the right attitude, every moment can be exciting.

Just living in the present can generate a level of excitement and be a good place to start. We are alive. We are breathing. Is this not exciting in itself? It's a good place to be. Having respect for your immediate environment and your current conditions sets a baseline for the future and for developing plans for it. If we can cherish these simple moments, we can thrill to experiencing the rewards of being alive, breathing in the morning air and smelling a new dawn.

For me, part of the excitement of life was being a racing sailor. I enjoyed racing both small, one-design boats on inland lakes in Ohio, as well as larger boats in Lake Erie's deep-water races. I remember the details of preparing for the start of a morning regatta, the ripples on the water indicating the speed and direction of the wind, and the patches of clouds that forecast heavier conditions to come. I experienced a sense of calm as our boat was launched and resting on the water, while knowing this calm would soon be shattered by the starting gun and the confusion of thirty to fifty boats competing to be first across the starting line. As we approached the starting line, my heart would begin beating faster. I knew that every decision, every tweak of the tiller would be crucial to our position in the first leg of the race. And while we were planning our approach, we were always aware of the potential dangers of boats racing within a few feet of each other with a collision possible at any moment.

Many people think about sailing as a relaxing experience, and it can be, but not in racing. Whether you are in a two-hour race around the buoys or a twenty-four-hour race around the islands, every moment is exciting. Your heart beats faster at the starting line, overtaking another boat is a thrill, and reaching the marker first is a cause for celebration.

When we raced, we were 100% there in the now. We were alive, and we were experiencing every ounce of the excitement of the moment – waves crashing against the hull, the wind in the sails, the challenge of launching the spinnaker on the downwind legs, the thrill of winning. Those were some of the most exciting times I ever experienced, and I remember them fondly.

We can find excitement in many sports, but we can also find excitement in activities that may not seem exciting to others or from the outside. One of the many gifts that I have been given is the ability to play the piano and enjoy music. When I began as an eight-year-old, learning the scales and the value of notes and chords on the musical staff, I really didn't understand what was to come. It was a routine without emotion, without a sense of connecting relationships, a mechanical process, one note after the other without feeling or expression. However, as I matured in my learning, I began to experience a deeper understanding – one that connected musical progressions with life experiences, with memories of cherished occasions, with people, with loving relationships.

Suddenly playing music became an exciting experience. It had more meaning than just the mechanical progression of notes. It involved emotional expression and fond memories of the past, revived in the progression of musical passages. Playing music became an exciting experience filled with emotion, touched by cherished relationships and all evolving from the notes on the piano that portrayed a history of my life, experienced, once again, in the musical score being played. To this day, playing the piano engages all my senses. I hear the notes, feel the thrill of the musical sound, and experience the music eliciting emotions. I have been very lucky to experience this type of excitement.

My mother wanted me to play the piano when I was a young boy. And, of course, I wanted to please my mother. We had a very close relationship. My father died on my first birthday, so she was my only parent as I was growing up. Week after week, year after year, she would take me to my piano lessons. Scale after scale. Mistake after mistake, she listened as I progressed. After nine years of practice and lessons, I finally completed the course of study and was able to play the finest of classical composers and feel the thrill and excitement of their compositions just as they did when their music was written and performed in the great concert halls of Europe. And, still, many decades later, music brings back wonderful memories of family, friends, school and college, concerts and musicals. My mother died when I was nineteen, but her memory lives on within me as I play the piano, pieces that I played for her many years ago. A gentle excitement. A respectful excitement. But, in the end, a deep excitement filled with meaning, memories and joy.

We all have fond memories, which are the only memories worth having. Being positive about our past means that we focus on fond relationships and warm experiences. Excitement can be the thrill of watching your favorite sports team strive for the win, seeing a Broadway chorus reach a crescendo or experiencing a meaningful and gentle moment with another. However we define excitement, we need to live within it, respect every moment, see the good in all of our experiences and enjoy the life we have been given.

Having a respect for life will help generate a level of excitement in all our experiences. We cannot waste one moment, because every moment in our life is a precious gift. To live with the thrill of anticipation and involve all our senses in every experience will enhance the excitement of the day. Every element in our life is alive, every action has meaning, and we have the opportunity to experience each encounter with an enhanced level of excitement. If we commit to it, our life can be as dramatic as a Broadway musical, as thrilling as quarterbacking the Super Bowl or as exciting as skippering a yacht in the America's Cup. Dream it. Be there. Live every moment with excitement.

Without leaps of imagination, or dreaming, we lose the excitement of possibilities.

—Gloria Steinem

UNLEASH YOUR FEELINGS: TWELVE STEPS

1. What gives you pleasure?
2. What brings you joy and happiness?
3. What inspires you?
4. What makes you thrilled and excited?
5. What feelings motivate you?
6. Who do you know that is positive and optimistic?
7. What are you looking forward to?
8. What places or experiences make you feel good?
9. What prompts you to have negative feelings or to feel discouraged?
10. What accomplishments make you feel excited and enthusiastic?
11. What could you change to reinforce your desired feelings?
12. How to you want to feel on a regular basis?

UNLEASH YOUR FEELINGS WORKSHEET

You have read the chapters about opening your mind, unleashing your imagination, and thinking about your feelings. Now it's time to identify what brings excitement and satisfaction to your life now or could do so in the future. The following questions will help you discover what is most important to your future.

List the important ways you want to feel in life.

1. _____

2. _____

3. _____

4. _____

5. _____

List what you could add to your life to reinforce your desired feelings.

1._____

2._____

3._____

4._____

5._____

List tasks and activities to delete from your life to support your desired feelings.

1._____

2._____

3._____

4._____

5._____

What types of things bring excitement and enthusiasm to your life?

1._____

2._____

3._____

4._____

5._____

Identify positive and optimistic people who inspire and motivate you.

1._____

2._____

3._____

4._____

5._____

List the happiest moments in your life.

1._____

2._____

3._____

4._____

5._____

List places and experiences that make you feel good and bring joy and happiness to your life.

1._____

2._____

3._____

4._____

5._____

Of all the answers above, select the three most important and list them below. Write them as an action statement. Example: I intend to live my life having congenial and peaceful relationships with people, and I plan to reevaluate my relationships with friends and associates based on their compatibility with my desired feelings.

1._____

2._____

3._____

four

DISCOVER YOUR PURPOSE

DESCRIBE YOUR INTERESTS & TALENTS

I know of no single formula for success. But… some attributes of leadership are universal and are often about finding ways of encouraging people to combine their efforts, their talents, their insights, their enthusiasm and their inspiration to work together.

—Queen Elizabeth II

IN THE FIRST THREE CHAPTERS you have worked to discover your most important feelings as you identified your dreams and aspirations. This chapter guides you through a close look at yourself, determining who you really are, what you believe in and what your guiding principles are. Are you who you want to be or who someone else wants you to be? This question may seem strange, but as you investigate your true self, you may find things you do based on someone else's desires, not yours, but perhaps the wishes of your parents, your spouse, a religious leader or a teacher who was a significant influence. What you really want to know is what you believe, what motivates you, and what your interests are.

To achieve success in life, it's crucial to do what you really enjoy and are dedicated to. When you know what your interests are, you can integrate them into your life's work, and when you spend your time, that essential currency of life, on what you believe is important and what you love to do, that is success.

We each were born with specific DNA that sets the stage for our personality, preferences, and interests. Some of us enjoy participating in athletics, some prefer the arts, while others are fascinated with technology, mathematical equations or researching new phenomena. We are all unique, and it is vital to understand and exploit what makes us unique. In addition to unique interests, we are blessed with certain talents entwined with these interests or that we chose to practice until we became proficient. Interests and talents have a way of entering our life by accident, so it is best to ensure that they are truly our own.

Let's begin by making out a list of things that interest you. Interests may be activities you find pleasurable or something you want to achieve. Look at the list below, answer the questions and enjoy finding out more about yourself:

1. List the activities that are most fun and interesting to you.
2. List the people that you enjoy and feel most comfortable with.
3. List the places you like to go in your free time.
4. List the hobbies that are most exciting for you.
5. List the types of books you enjoy or the research areas that are of most interest.
6. List your most favorite vacation destinations.
7. List various new things or activities that you think you would like to try doing.
8. List places you would like to visit or learn more about.

Often our interests and talents are congruent. However, sometimes our talents are limited and inhibit us from pursuing specific interests. As you have matured, you have acquired certain talents. These may have to do with your profession, or they may be more focused on your hobbies and leisure time. It is important to know what you are truly good at doing, whether it is playing in sports, giving oral presentations, working on highly technical mathematical equations, developing new inventions, or creating artwork. If your interests and your talents coincide, that is wonderful. If not, then you may need to make some choices.

Review the list below, answer the questions and find out more about your talents and skills:

1. List your most important personal talents.
2. List your professional talents, such as technical writing, leadership, organization, finance, creative expression, etc.
3. List your creative and cultural talents in music, art, theater, writing, public speaking, etc., or in developing creative and imaginative concepts.
4. List your athletic talents such as golf, tennis, bicycling, etc.
5. List your intellectual and analytical talents such as research, long-document writing, speed-reading, problem solving, designing products and systems, etc.
6. List your personality talents while communicating and interacting with people.
7. List your motivational talents in selling, teaching, leadership, and management.

Compare your two sets of lists. Do you find some commonality between items in each list? If so, that is terrific. We work best when we are interested in the work we do and when we find work that is directly tied to our overall mission and purpose in life. If our interests support the work we do and the leisure we enjoy, our chances of success are magnified. Additionally, if our interests are supported by our talents, this is an additional bonus.

When your interests and talents align with your values, your beliefs, and your purpose, and when your mission and goals are congruent with your actions, your life will be in harmony, and you will have achieved praxis. This is when you have a good chance at achieving a dynamic life. Eric Hoffer says, "We are told that talent creates its own opportunities. But it sometimes seems that intense desire creates not only its own opportunities, but its own talents."

Everything needs to be in alignment. A career that is not congruent with your interests and talents is just a job. To find excitement in your career, it must be passionately driven by your interests and talents. Working at something that you are marginally good at will not get you to where you want to be. You cannot bring the best of your abilities to such a job. Your abilities or educational background might not be well suited to it, but even if it is, not having a passion for your work creates a dissonance in life. What we want to achieve is a harmonious relationship in our interests, abilities, and career, whatever it is. Go with your interests. Go with your passion. Go with what is really exciting to you. Then you will be able to give it your all, and your chances of success will be magnified.

Knowing yourself is key. Being honest about your reality is essential. Connecting your interests and talents with your actions is indispensable to a successful career and important in personal relationships and leisure time activities. Do what you feel deeply about and are most interested in, and don't sacrifice your interests. They are what you are all about. They are what developed your personality. The more connected your interests and talents are to your professional and personal activities, the more joy and well-being you will bring to your life.

A winner is someone who recognizes his God-given talents, works his tail off to develop them into skills, and uses these skills to accomplish his goals.

—Larry Bird

IDENTIFY YOUR VALUES & PRINCIPLES

Economic prosperity may come and go; that's just how it is. But values are the steady currency that earns us the all-important rewards of self-respect and peace of mind.

—Peter Buffet

What do you stand for? What do you want to contribute to society? How do you want to support the issues that are important to you? How can you create a perfect life—one that is driven by a purpose and meaning? These are the questions we all struggle with as we think about our life and the decisions we make on a daily basis. But how do we find answers to these questions? I spent much of my professional life teaching design students how to strive for excellence in their research and design projects. I have also worked with hundreds of businesses, helping in their marketing efforts. Even after these intense experiences, I still need to ask myself these same questions. We all get caught in the routine and patterns of our past and constantly get drawn back into the rut of our responsibilities. Joey Reiman in his book *Thinking for a Living* says, "Do you know what happens to people who get into a groove? The groove becomes a rut, and the rut becomes a grave." Have you ever heard someone described as "buried in work"? Don't let that be you. Break away from routine before it buries you in unimportant tasks.

Who are we? What are our beliefs, our values, and our principles? These make up character and personality. Brian Tracey, in *Focal Point,* presents a strong list of values to review. John Nelson and Richard Bolls, in *What Color Is Your Parachute,* provide a test that clarifies, numerically, one's most important values. Darren Hardy, the publisher of *Success Magazine* and the author of *The Compound Effect,* also focuses on self-understanding and personal evaluation. Each of these authors believe understanding one's values is paramount.

I found that knowing my values is essential to refining my beliefs, establishing principles for living and eventually defining my purpose. As I made my selection of values, I prioritized them and developed the following list. It was difficult to choose three top values, so I followed the short list with a second tier of values that are also high priority. Here are the results of my discovery.

TOP THREE PERSONAL VALUES

Excellence in Beauty and Design

Happiness

Peace

MORE HIGH-PRIORITY PERSONAL VALUES

Creativity	Truthfulness	Politeness
Organization	Imagination	Sincerity
Good Manners	Ambition	Self-Discipline
Wisdom	Honesty	Courtesy
Achievement	Self-Direction	Warmth

PRINCIPLES

As I reviewed all my important values, it became clearer how I could define the principles by which I live and interact with people. I have an unwavering respect for beauty in all its forms and applications. I'm sure this has been central to my long career as a professor of art and in the teaching of design principles to thousands of students. I have a high regard for positive psychology, optimism, and happiness. I only have one life, and I am doing everything I can to fill it with happiness and joy. I require only peaceful relationships with friends and associates. I was trained as a classical pianist, and I know only too well what is meant by dissonance. For me to be happy, harmony, including peaceful relationships with friends, family, and business associates, must be a constant. These are the principles I live by.

PURPOSE

My purpose in life is to promote beauty and design excellence and to be a positive influence on the lives of others through my writing, public speaking, design work and paintings. It is my goal to improve the lives of millions of people by influencing them to unleash their imagination and help them create spectacular lives. This is stated quite simply, but it has taken years of research and self-understanding to come to this point. It is a very rewarding place to be—to understand who I am, why I am and what my purpose in life is.

A logical series of steps can foster your self-understanding and eventually shape your philosophy. By following these steps, you can discover your own set of values, which can guide you to developing your principles, purpose, and philosophy. Too many people begin by listing their goals without really understanding why they have chosen these goals. Through a process of discovering your values and defining your philosophy, you will have a more authentic rationale for proceeding to your mission and goals.

1. Undertake research and discovery
2. Determine your values
3. Refine and articulate your beliefs
4. Define your principles
5. Determine your life's purpose
6. Formulate your philosophy
7. Develop your mission in life
8. Establish your goals
9. Develop an action plan
10. Implement your plan

Let's hunt for the values you might embrace. Select from the list below to determine which are important to you. Then prioritize the top three, four or five. This should be revealing and start you on your journey to creating your life principles and purpose.

Accuracy	Benevolence	Dependability
Achievement	Calmness	Devotion
Adventure	Caring	Education
Aesthetics	Compassion	Empathy
Affection	Confidence	Excellence
Ambition	Conscientious-	Fairness
Aspiration	ness	Faithfulness
Authenticity	Courage	Forgiving
Authority	Courtesy	Friendliness
Balance	Creativity	Gentleness
Beauty	Daring	Good Manners

Gratitude	Loyalty	Self-Direction
Happiness	Optimism	Self-Discipline
Harmony	Orderliness	Sensitivity
Health	Organization	Sincerity
Hedonism	Originality	Sociability
Helpfulness	Patience	Spirituality
Honesty	Peacefulness	Strength
Hope	Personability	Stability
Humility	Pleasantness	Success
Humor	Pleasure	Sympathy
Imagination	Politeness	Thoughtfulness
Impartiality	Power	Tradition
Independence	Precision	Tranquility
Innovation	Professionalism	Trustworthiness
Integrity	Quality	Truthfulness
Intelligence	Respect	Vigor
Joy	Responsibility	Wisdom
Kindness	Safety	Wealth
Knowledge	Security	Youthfulness
Leadership	Self-Actualization	
Love	Self-Control	

Use this list as a guide, and feel free to add to it. Your list of values can be quite extensive and grow deeper in specific areas. This list is a good starting point from which to begin your journey.

Selecting your most important values should begin to reveal the qualities in life you stand for, and that guide your preferences and direct your actions. From these selections, you should be able to begin developing the principles that guide your life. Ask yourself, "How do I live by these values?" Try to transform your values into a statement of principles, keeping in mind that one statement of principle may incorporate several values. Write out these principles and see how they relate to your most important values. Once these have been written, see if they can guide you to understanding your life's purpose. These three, values, principles, and purpose, are all connected, of course. Each reinforces the other and by comparing them, you will have a wonderful understanding of how your values, philosophy and purpose are working in unison and how your beliefs and actions are congruent and reinforcing each other.

DEFINE YOUR BELIEFS

If you take the time to figure out your purpose in life, I promise that you will look back on it as the most important thing you will have ever learned.

—Clayton Christensen

When you meet people in your business or social gatherings, they might ask the question, "Tell me about yourself." Typically, you would answer by telling them where you work, where you went to school, your hometown, the name of your spouse and how many children you have. But is that who you really are? We are more than our hometown, our favorite high school or college courses, and what our children are doing. We have personal passions for living. We have philosophical priorities for why we are living and what makes us get up in the morning with excitement and enthusiasm. These are called our beliefs. Our beliefs are more important than our resume or our biography because they really divulge our deep personal philosophy. They help to identify the "why" in our lives – why we make decisions, why we decide to pursue a specific activity, and who we become friends with.

Our beliefs are driven by our values and help define our philosophy. All of this forms our purpose and mission in life. While thinking about this, I decided to make an attempt to identify my personal beliefs and found the process fascinating, because it made me go much deeper into thinking about my philosophy and values. Rather than listing the places I wanted to visit or things I wanted to do (the typical bucket list), I listed my beliefs.

I believe:

1. We are surrounded by beauty, and that it is our responsibility to share all the beauty we can with the world.
2. Promoting peace is critical to making the world a better place.
3. Education is the most important tool in advancing our life and our civilization.
4. We should be excited about life and thrilled to be alive.
5. Learning and the quest for self-improvement are lifelong.
6. We are responsible for our life, and we need to take control of our activities in order to support our ultimate goal.
7. Living a spiritual life is best, one which cherishes our existence, respects the complexity of human life, and is awed by the unknown.

These are some of the beliefs important to my life. They help me make decisions in my daily activities and focus my thinking on my ultimate goal. Identifying our beliefs is one of the critical components of congruency – where our thoughts and activities are in alignment and work together to support our philosophy.

BUILD YOUR PHILOSOPHY

I marveled at the beauty of all life and savored the power and possibilities of my imagination. In these rare moments, I prayed, I danced, and I analyzed. I saw that life was good and bad, beautiful and ugly. I understood that I had to dwell on the good and beautiful in order to keep my imagination, sensitivity, and gratitude intact. I know it would not be easy to maintain this perspective. I know I would often twist and turn, bend and crack a little, but I also know that...I would never completely break.

—Maria Nhambu

What is so important to you that you would dedicate your life to enhancing its importance and making it a success? I know there are causes important to you, charities in need of your expertise and issues deep seated in your conscious or subconscious mind that cause you to make certain decisions, guiding your actions and commitments. Your philosophy is the most personal summary of all these qualities. It is unique and reflective of only you, driven by your beliefs and interests and guided by your principles and values. But forming your philosophy is not easy, because to articulate your philosophy, to live by it and embrace it as your guide, you truly need to understand who you are.

The word "philosophy" comes from ancient Greek and literally means "love of wisdom." It often refers to the study of knowledge or, simply, thinking about thinking. The seven branches of philosophy are metaphysics, epistemology, anthropology, ethics, logic, political science, and aesthetics. According to the *Encyclopedia Britannica*, philosophy is "the rational, abstract, and methodical consideration of reality as a whole or of fundamental dimensions of human existence and experience." More casually put, philosophy is one's overall vision of or attitude toward life and the purpose of life.

At the end of this chapter, you will be asked to answer a series of questions all of which lead to writing your philosophy. Writing your philosophy must be influenced by and include your most critical beliefs, your most important values, and those principles central to your life.

As you have gathered by now, I am driven by supporting the arts and culture in our society. I believe that the visual and performing arts enhance our quality of life, free our imagination and stimulate our creativity. Integrated with music and often with a story, they create a complex stimulus which can develop a mood of relaxation, excitement, spirituality, or peaceful tranquility. To me, the arts and various forms of cultural expression are an important source of inspiration for the enjoyment of life. They are imaginative, creative, and evocative, not analytical or rational. The drama of *Les Misérables*, the soothing refrains of a Bach prelude, the poetry of Shakespeare, the visual depth of Rubens' paintings or the three-dimensional excitement of a Frank Gehry building all play with our senses, set a mood, and allow us to experience something inspiring.

To me, life has been a wonderful experience. I believe in the goodness of mankind. I believe we have a common bond as citizens of a great society. We share, we give, we contribute to the quality of life for our fellow man. I approach life with a very positive and optimistic spirit, knowing that, in the end, it will all be fine. Nothing is ever as bad as it might seem, and nothing is ever as good as it might seem. But somewhere in the middle, one can find joy and happiness.

Building your philosophy involves summarizing all that you are and all that is important to you. Building your new life with a sound understanding of your philosophy will give you a head start at creating a life that is exciting but also in harmony. You can bring your beliefs, values, principles, and philosophy into harmony with your actions. With this combination, you can reach a state of excellence in your life. Everyone's philosophy will, naturally, be widely diverse – all based upon life experiences, education, family history and a lifetime of other influences. Let me share a few quotations that express a series of diverse philosophies.

The formula of life is simple. It is the formula of giving – giving courage, attention, peace, love and comfort to yourself and the society.

—Amit Ray

I have never, in all my life, not for one moment, been tempted toward religion of any kind. The fact is that I feel no spiritual void. I have my philosophy of life, which does not include any aspect of the supernatural and which I find totally satisfying. I am, in short, a rationalist and believe only that which reason tells me is so.

—Isaac Asimov

Live your life in such a way that you'll be remembered for your kindness, compassion, fairness, character, benevolence, and a force for good who had much respect for life, in general.

—Germany Kent

Human evolution has two steps – from being somebody to being nobody, and from being nobody to being everybody. This knowledge can bring sharing and caring throughout the world.

—Sri Sri Ravi Shankar

Every man must have a philosophy of life, for everyone must have a standard by which to measure his conduct. And philosophy is nothing but a standard by which to measure.

—Bhimrao Ramji Ambedkar

There's no such thing as 'one, true way'; the only answers worth having are the ones you find for yourself; leave the world better than you found it. Love, freedom, and the chance to do some good – they're the things worth living and dying for.

—Mercedes Lackey

We have diverse philosophies because we are all different people. We are the sum of our experiences, and each of us has quite different experiences. Your philosophy must come from within, to paraphrase Stephen Covey. When your philosophy has come from deep inside you, it will be truly yours, strong enough to inspire a commitment to its purpose. As you begin to make changes in your life and develop a vision for your future, look to your values and beliefs, and make sure your new plan and the actions that will follow are derived from your philosophy.

DISCOVER YOUR GIFT

The secret of all greatness is to discover what you were born to do in life and then do it. You must find out your gifts and talents.

—Sunday Adelaja

Identifying all your talents and skills is essential to your self-discovery research. You might begin by listing your most important qualities and how they can have an impact. Ask yourself, "Why am I here and what do I do best?" Your questions and answers will continue to evolve as you work toward planning your future and determining what is really important. We all have wishes and desires, and we all want to contribute, but what is it that we can offer? We are influenced by all types of stimuli. Our family and friends all offer suggestions for how to live our lives, but how can we sort out these influences and allow our true gifts to emerge and our desired legacy to be clear?

Robin Wall Kimmerer provides us her answer to the question of how our gift can have a positive impact on others:

> The most important thing each of us can know is our unique gift and how to use it in the world. Individuality is cherished and nurtured, because, in order for the whole to flourish, each of us has to be strong in who we are and carry our gifts with conviction, so they can be shared with others.

We have discussed various ways to look deeper into our minds, to discover our desires and hopes, and to allow new concepts to enter our decision-making. Looking deep and finding connections in our interests and talents might help us to allow our true gifts to emerge. We have been given our life and our mind, and these are gifts we cherish. But if we can identify a certain knowledge and talent that needs to surface, we can be stronger and more effective. Our experiences throughout life have made us unique and given us an expertise that is truly our own. No one else has exactly this same expertise because we see life through the lenses of our own experience, and we focus through the influence of our own preferences and prejudices. We have fine-tuned our talents based on these past experiences and established a fresh outlook on life that is our own and no one else's. From these talents, skills, and experiences, we need to discover our gift and allow it to emerge as a significant influence on our future decisions.

Discovering and understanding your gift will culminate in defining your purpose, and your purpose can inform and direct a multitude of decisions about your goals and future actions. Once you know your gift, your special talents and purpose, you can share these with others. How can your gift be introduced to your daily routines both in your profession and in your personal life? How can your gift be directed so that it becomes a tool or a process that can help others and make a positive impact on their lives? Once you have identified your gift, you can hone your gift and share it.

Finding your gift is part of what you are studying in this book. Through self-analysis, you can look back on your history to see what were the most important influences in your life. You can determine the impact your education – in and out of the classroom – has had on your life and discover the beliefs and principles that guide your life.

Looking over my career and the interests and talents I have, how do I perceive my gift? How can I share my gift for the betterment of others? As I try to understand who I am and what my convictions are, I try to inspire others with my philosophy. Optimism and positive thinking are essential to me and to how I approach life. I see everything first with optimism and try to resolve issues with a "can do" attitude. As I write this book, I hope that my philosophy will emerge and have a significant influence on your life. I have a deep respect for the beauty that the arts contribute to life. Music, art, theater, literature, and design are all vital to my quality of life. My gift is to share my talents by creating paintings that inspire, music that stimulates, design that solves important problems, and writing that has a positive influence. It is essential to share my gifts because I know that sharing them will help others live an extraordinary life, a life filled with excitement, joy, and happiness.

What is your gift to share? What are your talents, interests and expertise and how can you give these gifts back to others? In *Finding Your Strength in Difficult Times: A Book of Meditations,*" David Viscott says, "The purpose of life is to discover your gift. The work of life is to develop it. The meaning of life is to give your gift away."

CLARIFY YOUR PURPOSE

If today were the last day of my life, would I want to do what I am about to do today? ...Your time is limited, so don't waste it living someone else's life.

—Steve Jobs

Victor Frankl, in *Man's Search for Meaning*, describes the unfathomable suffering that took place in the Nazi concentration camps. Millions were exterminated, yet Frankl survived. Certainly, luck was involved. But also involved was his will to live and his passion for purpose. In his book, Frankl quotes the German philosopher, Nietzsche: "He who has a why to live for can bear almost any how."

Thousands of books have been written about how to live your life, how to find happiness, how to be optimistic and how to succeed in business. Nietzsche and Frankl suggest a key to the motivation that directs our lives. Frankl believes that logotherapy is the process that will help people find their answers. "*Logos* is a Greek word which denotes 'meaning.' Logotherapy... focuses on the meaning of human existence as well as on man's search for such a meaning." This striving to find a meaning in one's life is the primary motivational force in man.

Why do we exist? What is our reason for living the life that we do? And what motivates us to choose the directions that we take in life? Most importantly, what is the underlying purpose in our life that guides our actions, our commitments and our most critical decisions?

In *The Infinite Game* Simon Sinek suggests that leaders should adopt an infinite perspective as they make decisions for their businesses. Too many leaders make decisions based on the crises of the moment and do not take on a long-term outlook. Daily decisions may have little to do with a company's most critical goals and ambitions and can often be a distraction that takes leaders off course and solves only the nagging problems of the day. He recommends that business leaders develop their most important commitment to what he calls their "Just Cause."

Sinek's philosophy is an excellent guide for business – to take a longer view and identify the most important cause that motivates our actions and drives our decisions. He suggests that every company should appoint a CVO (Chief Vision Officer) to monitor the process and help to keep leaders on track with their ultimate goal. This is an excellent concept and one that can provide an important leadership role for businesses. However, as I read his book, I saw that these concepts are not only important for businesses, but also important to us as individuals.

We can choose to accept a vision from another or to become the Chief Vision Officer for our own life. We need to identify our "Just Cause." Many philosophers recommend developing a vision for our lives and crafting that vision with the support of our values, belief,s and desires. As we develop our personal vision it will be influenced by our life's purpose – our "just cause." We need to look at our lives with a long-term perspective so that all the decisions we make from day to day support our most important cause. As we define the cause we are committed to, we can begin to understand the purpose that validates our existence and actions.

Frank Lloyd Wright has been called the greatest American architect or even the greatest of all time. I have studied Wright's architectural design and philosophy since my early days as a student and have a high regard for his philosophy and his marvelous architectural designs. Wright coined the term "Organic Architecture," as a definition of his design philosophy. He spent his life dedicated to this philosophy and leaves over a thousand examples of his innovative organic style. His is known for all types of architecture, but his most important contributions came in his residential designs. Wright says, "Let your home appear to grow easily from its site and shape it to sympathize with the surroundings if Nature is manifest there, and if not, try and be as quiet, substantial, and organic as she would have been if she had the chance."

He defined his architecture as appropriate – appropriate to time, appropriate to place and appropriate to people. He felt that the building should belong to the era in which it was created and that the building should be in harmony with its natural environment. He felt that the building's first mission was to serve its occupants.

Wright had a tremendous respect for beauty. I have visited both of his schools, Taliesin East and West, on many occasions and have studied his educational philosophy and design principles. His life and teachings were filled with an appreciation for culture – music, literature, theater, and art were all part of his influence on his students. He was dedicated to beauty. A mentor and teacher to thousands of students and professional architects and designers, Wright is as a fine example of one who was dedicated to a purpose, guided by principles, and reinforced by standards and values.

It's an exciting concept to think that every day, we could wake up with excitement and enthusiasm and with a purpose that reinforces all our actions. We need to define a vision that ignites our commitment to a cause – one driven by our life's purpose.

SEE YOUR MISSION AS A GIFT

Our life is not a problem to be solved, it is a gift to be opened.

—Wayne Muller

In *How, Then, Shall We Live?* Wayne Muller reflects on the importance of life and how precious it is to be alive. We have been given a gift, the gift of life. We only receive this gift once, and we have a responsibility to cherish it, develop it, nurture it and open it slowly with respect and wonder. Just think how important this gift is. While we all have this gift, each of our gifts is different, defined by our experiences, our talents, and our beliefs. Our gifts come with unique opportunities, and we are responsible for fulfilling those opportunities and allowing them to unfold as contributions to our society.

What does your gift look like? Is it an ability to understand complex relationships, be the teacher a child needs, engineer a safe structure, diagnose a patient, or design products to improve lives? We all have a purpose, and it starts with opening our gifts and seeing how they can make a difference. As Wayne Muller says,

Each day is an opportunity to say something honestly, to make something more beautiful, to create something precious, to give a gift only we can provide for the family of the earth. To dedicate a single act to the healing of others is a day well lived.

As a designer, artist, and educator, I was once asked to explain what my mission is in life. This is one of the most important questions anyone can answer. But before the answer can surface, we first need to understand who we are, what we value, and what we consider our purpose in life. Understanding these qualities is vitally important and well worth undertaking in your personal research. Consider how most corporations create a mission statement, often using similar words. In *The Mission Statement Book*, Jeffrey Abrahams lists the words most often and least often found in corporate mission statements:

Most Often Used Words	Least Often Used Words
Customers	Joy
Employees	Conscience
Growth	Goodwill
Environment	Passion
Profit	Exciting
Leader	Harmony
Respect	Enthusiasm
Commitment	
Communities	
Excellence	
Performance	
Goal	
Individual	
Innovation	

I was surprised to see the rarity of the words in the second column, all of which refer to the quality of life. They suggest the excitement and joy to be experienced while working toward the mission. As individuals, we can give these quality-of-life ideas more importance.

How would you write your mission statement? What is your mission in life? What gifts have you been given? As you write your mission statement, can you introduce words that reflect the qualities you wish to build into your life? You are the most important person in your life. You have the total responsibility of understanding who you are and what you believe. The most important project that you have in life is to design your life. Your life is not a problem to be solved, but a gift to be cherished, to be understood and to be realized. Everything is inside that gift, ready to be opened. You are important to this world. You have a gift ready to be shared. Find that gift. Harness your energies and make your contribution to your world. And enjoy the process that lies ahead.

To attain knowledge, add things every day. To attain wisdom, remove things every day.

—Tao Te Ching

WRITE YOUR CREED

I foresee a new kind of spiritual creativity, in which we no longer decide whether to believe in a given creed and follow a certain tradition blindly. This new religion is a blend of individual inspiration and inspiring tradition.

—Thomas Moore

What principles do you live by? You have already identified them in writing your core values, your beliefs, your life's purpose, and your personal philosophy. Is it possible to bring all this thinking together to make a single statement of belief in a personal life creed? This may take time and analysis, but the connections need to be made in order to develop a statement of your personal creed.

Each religion, fraternity and service club has a creed that governs the beliefs and actions of its followers. For example, Rotary International, the world's largest service organization, has what it calls the "Four Way Test." It asks the following four questions: "Of the things we think, say or do: Is it the truth? Is it fair to all concerned? Will it build goodwill and better friendships? Will it be beneficial to all concerned?"

As you write your own creed, refer to the creeds held by organizations to which you belong. These may be good models for your personal creed. But, because these other creeds do not embody your entire philosophy, use them only as a hint about your statement – choosing elements pertaining to your spiritual and philanthropic beliefs. The business you work for might have a creed or overall philosophy by which it does business. Parts of this creed may find its way into your personal creed. This is a process of connecting your most important values and integrating them into a single statement.

Here is my personal creed to follow as a potential model for your consideration:

- I believe in beauty and peace and in the importance of aesthetics in our world.
- I respect all living people.
- I believe in honesty and integrity in everything that I do and in all my communications.
- I hold truth and learning high in my esteem and am personally guided by the pursuit of excellence.

Your creed is the summary of who you are and a synthesis of your beliefs, your philosophy and your life's purpose. Create it and be guided by it throughout your life. Once you have done this, it makes your decisions much easier because you will be guided by these words.

The more we find ways to live our values on a daily basis, the more satisfied with our lives we'll be.

—M. J. Ryan

BE INSPIRED BY MEANING

When we perform work with the conviction that what we do matters, we can live intensely. Without a reason for moving forward, we have no drive. When we live intentionally – with a clear sense of why what we do matters – life has meaning and brings fulfillment.

—Jay Shetty

As I began writing this book, my objectives were to help you design a life that

- allows your dreams and aspirations to emerge.
- inspires you to develop innovative and meaningful daily work.
- brings excitement back into your life.
- helps you focus on developing a life with extraordinary ambitions and goals that exceed your current expectations.

I wanted to change people's lives by having them think optimistically, with an expectant attitude and a belief that they can make significant changes directed by their hopes and dreams for their future.

To accomplish this, I found that there was a progression of reasoning that needed to take place. To succeed in making ambitious decisions and working successfully toward achievements, each of us needs to adopt a series of beliefs. We need to

1. Believe in ourselves.
2. Believe that change is possible.
3. Believe that we can change.
4. Believe that we deserve to live a new life influenced by these changes.
5. Approach life with optimism and a positive attitude.
6. Believe that our dreams and desires are possible to accomplish.
7. Understand why we want to achieve our dreams and desires.
8. Believe that hope is possible.
9. Articulate our values and principles.
10. Approach our goals and aspirations with a sense of urgency.
11. Believe in a vision with ambitious expectations.
12. Believe that every decision and action we make is reinforced by meaning.

Changing your life is not simple. It cannot be accomplished by a single act. It takes a belief system that inspires confidence, an approach that is positive and a belief that anything is possible. It needs to be supported by reason and inspired by meaning.

Why do you want to change? Why do you want to relocate? Why do you need to change your relationships? There must be a reason, a reason driven by meaning in your life. Victor Frankl believes that "this striving to find a meaning in one's life is the primary motivational force in man." Your most important decisions need to be driven by meaning. Your decisions for change will be more successful if they are reinforced by understanding how they have a personal meaning in your life. Asking why for each of your questions will provide answers that support your decisions and actions. And asking why will allow you to form a plan for how to achieve them.

If we are passionate about the reason for taking an action or making a decision, we understand why we are making that decision and we are driven by the meaning it has in our life, we will have the motivation and drive to accomplish it and make it a successful venture. Without these influences, it will have less chance to succeed.

As you read, you will find that you need to make a commitment – to yourself, to your success, and to your happiness and joy. To create a dynamic new direction for your life, you need to believe in yourself. To leave the legacy you want, you need to be successful in this new direction. All of this comes, first, with an understanding of who you are, what you believe in, and what you are committed to. And to determine what these are, you need to see how each of your choices have a deep meaning in your life, to your values, and to your beliefs.

By answering the questions at the end of each chapter and filling out the lists, you will begin to build a composite of your beliefs and philosophy and understand what is meaningful to you. The more committed you are to answering the questions and making out your lists, the better the results will be and the greater chance that a deeper understanding of your life will be revealed.

Man is originally characterized by his 'search for meaning' rather than his 'search for himself.' The more he forgets himself—giving himself to a cause or another person—the more human he is. And the more he is immersed and absorbed in something or someone other than himself the more he really becomes himself.

—Victor E. Frankl

ASK WHY

The creative act itself is one of breaking from tradition and routine in order to create new patterns, ask new questions, and seek new answers. Creative people march to the beat of a different drummer—themselves!

—Scott Barry Kaufman

When you were a child, did you ever ask why? Of course, we all did – to the point that it drove our parents to a frenzy. But it is a very important question – why? Unfortunately, we too often act without asking this question, without understanding the real reasons that we engage in various activities or make certain decisions. Understanding our "why" must be the underpinning of everything we do and every decision we make.

Daydreaming and responding to our impulses are wonderful avenues for bringing our subconscious to the surface, but digging deeper to find out the reasons for our actions will bring us closer to our true core principles and provide direction for major decisions in our lives. Simon Sinek, in *Find Your Why*, provides a good way to understand how our 'why' is the most important element in communicating our message. Sinek's philosophy relates directly to one's business as well as one's personal life. He believes that "Happiness comes from what we do. Fulfillment comes from why we do it." In business, Sinek says, we are always promoting what we do and how we do it; unfortunately, we rarely mention why we do it. And yet, it is the why that tugs on the emotions and gives people a reason to buy our products or services, and in our personal life, reinforces and validates the actions we take.

In our search for authenticity in our lives, this principle is as important as it is in the world of business. We need to search for truth in our lives constantly and attempt to find reasons why we make certain decisions and take certain actions. Remember, what we do can bring happiness to our lives, but why we do it provides the meaning that validates our actions. When our beliefs and our actions are in alignment, we find congruency and praxis in our lives. If our beliefs and our actions are in alignment, happiness is the way; it is part of the process.

Once we have unleashed our imagination and allowed our dreams and desires to surface, we can start planning new directions for our lives. During the design process, it would be helpful to validate those directions and decisions by asking the question, "why." Asking this question can lead us to understanding the purpose for our lives and understanding our purpose uncovers the reasons for all our actions and decisions. Consider how your "why" fits into, reinforces and validates each of these categories:

- Your values
- Your beliefs
- Your philosophy
- Your life's purpose
- Your life's mission
- Your creed

Asking why is not easy. To be able to understand our "why," we need to understand how each decision we make connects with our basic principles, values, and beliefs. This could all be connected in a personal philosophical map that identifies each of the parts and pieces that we deem important. We have all heard of the concept of mind-mapping. This can be an effective process in making connections and being able to find relationships in our thought process. Consider creating a mind map of your feelings, your beliefs, and your personal values. Each of these elements are connected. Your life is a process. Understanding your beliefs takes soul searching, research and pursuing your own personal search for meaning. With an open mind, a vibrant curiosity, and a spirit of imagination, we can unleash those hidden dreams and desires and connect them with our life principles. It takes work and analysis, but it is worth it to be able to know who we really are, why we exist and what drives our actions.

The best scientists and explorers have the attributes of kids! They ask questions and have a sense of wonder. They have curiosity. 'Who, what, where, why, when and how!' They never stop asking questions, and I never stop asking questions, just like a five-year-old.

—Sylvia Earle

DISCOVER YOUR PURPOSE: TWELVE STEPS

1. List your interests.
2. Identify your talents and skills.
3. List your personal strengths.
4. Select your most important values.
5. Define your beliefs.
6. List the principles by which you live.
7. Select which traits are most important to you.
8. What gives your life meaning?
9. Define your philosophy.
10. Understand your life's purpose.
11. State your life's mission.
12. Write your personal creed.

DISCOVER YOUR PURPOSE WORKSHEET

You have read the chapters about opening your mind, unleashing your imagination, and thinking about your beliefs, values, principles, interests, and talents. Now, explore ways to take action on many of the decisions you have made.

What are you most interested in and excited about?

1._____

2._____

3._____

4._____

5._____

What are your most important talents, skills, and strengths?

1._____

2._____

3._____

4._____

5._____

What are your most important values, beliefs, and principles?

1._____

2._____

3._____

4._____

5._____

What causes, relationships, and experiences give your life meaning?

1._____

2._____

3._____

4._____

5._____

Which of your values and beliefs should be part of your life's purpose?

1._____

2._____

3._____

4._____

5._____

Guided by your purpose, what should be included in your life's mission?

1._____

2._____

3._____

4._____

5._____

What should be included in your personal creed?

1._____

2._____

3._____

4._____

5._____

In the space below write three statements defining your life's purpose, mission, and creed. Example: My purpose is to contribute to the advancement of the arts and to work for supporting education in the arts at all levels.

1. Purpose: _____

    _____

    _____

2. Mission: _____

    _____

    _____

3. Creed: _____

    _____

    _____

five

UNDERSTAND YOUR CURRENT REALITY

ACCEPT RESPONSIBILITY

Work on yourself more than you do on your job.

—Jim Rohn

IN THE RESEARCH I HAVE DONE over the past several decades, I have listened to and read about the philosophies of leading psychologists, designers, philosophers, architects, futurists, and self-improvement advocates. Many of them directed their thoughts to business leaders and many were personal development advocates. I concluded that whatever the intent, there are principles that businesses and individuals share. In this book, I encourage you to unchain your curiosity, use your imagination to think deeply, and allow your hopes, dreams, and desires to surface. In order to do this, and with the support of dozens and dozens of supportive philosophies, think about the following statements, as held by many thought leaders.

1. We are all influenced by the routines and patterns of our current reality.
2. We are responsible for our own lives.
3. We can design our own life and our own future.
4. To change our life, we need to believe in our right to create a new life.

5. We need to be open, honest and willing to make changes to our current reality.
6. We need to create a vision for our future.
7. We need to set goals that are aspirational.
8. We need to have faith in achieving our new vision.
9. We need to take action to be able to accomplish our vision.
10. We need to believe in ourselves, our abilities and our right to pursue and succeed in our vision for a new reality.

Buckminster Fuller advocates many of these principles as he talks about creating a new life model that makes our existing model obsolete. Shawn Achor believes, "if you want to create positive change in your life, you first have to change your reality." Dr Wayne Dyer says, "You elevate your life by taking responsibility for who you are and what you're choosing to become."

These great thinkers advocate that you take responsibility to make your own decisions and to guide the future of your life. This is a reality that I hope you all can embrace. You can take responsibility and re-imagine your future, re-design your life and become excited about the possibilities of your future reality. As Albert Einstein said, "If you want to live a happy life, tie it to a goal, not to people or objects."

RESEARCH AND DISCOVER

Why focus on a question when what we really crave is an answer? It's simple. Answers come from questions, and the quality of any answer is directly determined by the quality of the question.

—Gary Keller

Coming from a background in advertising and design, I know that research and discovery are essential to developing an understanding of our clients, their products or services, their competition, and their selling environment. Advertising is not just creative guesswork. It involves doing research, collecting data, and understanding the client's product, services, and competition. Market timing, positioning and strategic media scheduling for campaigns become essential parts of the planning process – all based on sound data and research. Often, agencies are selected because of their experience in the client's field. Having that experience, the agency is well informed and has already laid some of the groundwork. They will have formed a good understanding of the unique characteristics of the industry and its consumers and will have established a working relationship with industry service providers and media partners.

Over many years, my company developed expertise in the kitchen and bath industries. As part of our work for several nationally known clients in these industries, we attended the major tradeshows, formed alliances with shelter magazines and building industry trade journals, toured factories, and interviewed sales staff, division managers and CEOs. In addition, we listened to our clients' customers and understood their preferences and reasons for buying. We wrote articles, press releases, placed advertising, coordinated photography sessions, and produced some of the most beautifully designed brochures, catalogs, and websites in the industry. To do that, we had to learn about what our clients were selling, where they were selling and who they were selling to. And we needed to understand the primary influences on customers' buying decisions. We needed to discover everything we could about the entire process from manufacturing and selling to the buying experience.

Our experience in marketing communications has its parallels in other professions. For example, in the legal profession, research and discovery are absolutely required. The discovery process begins with an attorney undertaking the required research to find out all that he or she can about a client, the facts surrounding the case, the people involved, the precedents set by similar cases, police reports and all other relevant information. This information is vital for preparing a case for a trial, and a similar process guides the preparation of corporate records and personal legal documents.

When an architect or structural engineer begins the process of designing for a client, the discovery process is just as important as it is for any other business where problem-solving is involved. If the structure being designed is a commercial building, the designer uses discovery to understand the client, the budget, and the clients' business, including how many people will be working in or visiting the building, job responsibilities, the possibility of future expansion, production facility requirements, special lighting and HVAC requirements, safety concerns and OSHA demands. Research is done to understand structural systems and building codes. And these are only some of the questions that need answers before the design process begins. All of this research and discovery comes well before a visual concept or mechanical detailing for the building has begun. Gaining this knowledge is essential to designing a safe, efficient and effective work environment. The process of research and discovery is a requirement in all the design professions.

This is true in medicine as well. Can you imagine your doctor giving you a diagnosis before doing a thorough examination and conversing about your symptoms and concerns? Of course not. And if it was the way he worked, you would have many suspicions about the diagnosis being made. No one can make decisions without research and discovery, and certainly not when it applies to your health.

Martin Seligman, writing in *Flourish*, discusses the importance of research and understanding oneself:

> Self-awareness involves reflection and introspection to gain insight into life's pressing questions. These questions pertain to identity, purpose, meaning, truth in the world, being authentic, creating a life worth living and fulfilling one's potential.

How can research and discovery apply to you and your life? As you read this book, I will challenge you to find out as much as you can about yourself and suggest pathways to discovery. I hope you can look at your life, evaluate it and make the necessary changes that will provide you with an extraordinary new future. I believe you can do this through a progression of actions within the design process. By following the exercises in this book, you can re-think your current life and make modest or aggressive changes to your current reality in order to reach your vision for a preferred future. In *How Will You Measure Your Life*, Clayton M. Christensen writes, "The type of person you want to become – what the purpose of your life is – is too important to leave to chance. It needs to be deliberately conceived, chosen and managed."

The first step in this process is to sense that something is not quite working to its maximum potential in your current reality. What is making you anxious, uncomfortable, unfulfilled, or maybe even angry? These feelings need to be recognized, so you can face them head on, determine why they are problems and find a way to change their impact on your life. You may need to ignore, minimize, or solve these problems before you can freely design your new vision. This is what I want for you. I want you to face the facts and understand fully where you are in life, in your relationships and in your profession. I want you to understand your current reality through appropriate research and discovery and be able to approach your life redesign with accuracy, authority, and confidence. Designing your life needs to be done with the same process used by the designer, architect, attorney, or physician. They all have a process, and it begins with doing the proper research and discovery. Look beyond your assumptions about your current problems and see what you can discover through research. Accuracy is vital. This is your life, and you are the one who will be making the decisions for change. You are in control of the process.

If you don't know what you want, something is stopping you from knowing it. Something – a hidden resistance – is making you hesitate to find your true desire and go after it. I would like you to find that resistance so you can figure out how to melt it.

—Barbara Sher

UNCOVER THE PROBLEMS

Before you can do something new, you have to stop doing something old.

—Peter Drucker

I'm a designer, and designers are problem solvers. That is our objective. Find the problem and fix it, make it better, make it work, or make it communicate better. Designers are found in a multitude of industries – design engineers, interior designers, industrial designers, systems designers, structural designers, graphic designers, product designers – and we all share similar processes: find the problems and fix them.

An interior designer, upon starting an assignment to design working or living spaces for a client, needs to find out as much as possible about the client and how the spaces are to be used. How can the spaces reinforce and support the client's function? What are the privacy needs of the occupants? How do the occupants want to feel while living or working in the newly designed spaces? What are their functions? What are their needs for special requirements such as natural light, balanced lighting, or acoustical controls? What are the problems in their client's current environments? The list of questions can be extensive, but the more they know about their client, the better their material selections and design solutions will be. They need to fully understand the problems and requirements of the project. This is a process of discovery, and through discovery many problems come to the surface.

The function of the graphic designer is to communicate and promote a client's products or services. In some cases, it is to provide information or instructions. This may include introducing a product, establishing an identity for the product or an emotional attitude toward it (branding), teaching the public how to buy or use it and explaining why they should do so. To do that, the designer needs to learn as much as possible about the product or service. How does it function? Where is it vis-à-vis the competition? Are there problems with the product? Does the product have unique advantages? Is the price a problem? Should the product be positioned as top, middle, or low quality? What will the product do for the user? Will it save time? Will it be less expensive in the long run? To design effective communication tools, a designer needs to know as much as possible about the product or service, the potential buyer and how to connect the two. When marketing research is successful, it often discovers a "pain point," a physical or psychological need that a product or service can meet. Addressing this "pain," weakness or blind spot can be compelling. It can overcome a buyer's natural resistance to taking action.

As you embark upon re-designing your life and re-shaping your future, search for what stopped you from moving forward in the past. What stood in your way then and may still stand in your way? Look for a personal pain point, a need, weakness, or blind spot. Your responsibilities, the people around you, a lack of desire, the presence of health issues, conflicting ambitions or other barriers may continually hold you back from making decisions or taking action. The design process can be an effective tool as you approach this research.

Let's look at how you can use the design process to re-design your life. But first you need to ask yourself why you want to re-design your life. What's wrong with it the way it is? I don't know the answer to this question, but you do. And if you don't, then you need to find out.

Finding effective answers to a problem is often a matter of asking the right questions. If you ask the wrong questions, you are going to follow a path that may have little to do with the real problems you are experiencing. Understanding the problems you face is very similar to asking the right questions. What really is standing in your way of living an extraordinary life? Who discourages you from achieving your most important ambitions? What conditions inhibit you from charging forward? These questions need to be answered honestly. If there are people who stand in your way, move away from them – literally or emotionally. If job requirements are not in harmony with your values, identify those problems and decide to change them. If you lack the appropriate advanced degree or special training to advance in your profession, make time to get that degree or training. You probably know what is holding you back. Dig deep and identify the problems. You will need to end, modify, or learn to ignore these problems before you can reach the point of freedom – freedom to choose your own new life.

We all begin by living a life someone else designed for us. We are expected to listen to our parents and teachers and do as they say. And we should continue to listen to the recommendations of the teachers in our lives, but they should not make decisions that guide our life. All too often, what our parents and teachers told us was out of date or wrong all along, but unfortunately, lessons learned early are hard to shake. Instead of taking all such lessons to heart, sort out the positive influences and integrate them into your life. Be guided first and foremost by your vision for yourself.

Ask the right questions. Identify the problems. Define the process for eliminating or modifying the problems and free yourself to choose your new life, the life that you will design. As in previous chapters, this chapter ends with a series of question and lists to complete. They can help you identify the barriers you face and have a better idea of what changes you want to make in your life.

Identify the routine tasks and activities that consume so much time but contribute little or nothing to your long-term goals.

—Brian Tracy

CONFRONT OBSTACLES

When you imagine that you're free of any need to use excuses, you'll ultimately act on what you're imagining. So practice the process of envisioning precisely what your life would look and feel like if it were impossible to enlist your excuse patterns. A good way to begin is by getting accustomed to visualizing exactly who you are, as if you've already arrived.

—Wayne Dyer

Pain. Pleasure. Obstacles. Opportunities. How can we strike a happy balance in our lives when so many factors influence our decisions? We try to reach a state of well-being, contentment, and happiness, but can we really get there if obstacles constantly drag us to a place where it is difficult to create a vision of our magnificent future? So, before we can make progress at re-building our lives and developing a plan, we need to have a clear view of where we are and what obstacles stand in our way of making progress. We cannot freely begin making plans for our future until we reach a place where we can think without the restrictions of negative influences. Arthur Schopenhauer, the German philosopher, advocated not trying to increase our happiness, but instead trying to diminish the misery in our lives. Whether it is misery, pain, obstacles, threats, or our own resistance to progress, before we can embark upon a new future and new vision for our lives, we need to confront the difficulties we face, identify them, and determine a clear path to a resolution.

Barbara Sher writes, in *I Could Do Anything If I Only Knew What It Was*, "To cause real change you must realize that there's a good reason for your problem – and find that reason. Then you'll be in a position to fix it." Problems and obstacles do not come by accident. There is usually a reason for their existence. So, as Sher indicates, we need to understand why the problem exists, determine how it became a problem and then, map out a strategy to eliminate or ameliorate it. Before we can begin to set goals and plan for our future, we need to gather information about obstacles. It is heartbreaking to set a goal and find that you have no way to achieve it with all the hurdles in the way. Consequently, while we need to dream and create a vision, we must confront the current reality, solve its problems, and then plan a future with unrestricted goals, developing a detailed process for reaching those goals.

First envision, then demolish barriers, then build. The best way to begin a design project is to start with a fresh sheet of paper for creating your vision. The best way to redesign a room is to empty it – at least mentally – and begin from blank walls. Understanding and eliminating the obstacles – at least mentally – will allow you to imagine freely, dream, and construct your wonderful concepts. But it is difficult to find that fresh paper, those blank walls, when your current life comes with an enormous amount of negativity.

Remember, in the first chapter, when you put your lists of problems in your lowest desk drawer? You need to clear the slate. Erase all those obstacles that conflict with your dreams and aspirations. Get to that zero point where most of those negative influences are put aside, modified, changed, or eliminated from your life. Or, if ignoring them is all you can do, determine to ignore them with firmness and without a shadow of guilt. It's not just people and things that get in the way. Each of us have unique, personal behaviors and habits that cause us to act as we do and govern the schedules of our day. These need to be reviewed.

Do you continue doing the same things, or do you make the hard choice to give up what gets you into trouble? Brian Tracey, the author of *Focal Point*, feels that a habit does not go away until it is replaced by a new habit. So, this means we need to do some clear thinking about how to satisfy that formula. Once you identify habits that are obstacles and you reschedule your day, you can begin to imagine and design a life that will bring you the excitement, achievements and pleasures you desire.

Understanding the difference between where you are and where you want to be, requires only a simple formula.

1. Develop a clear understanding of your current conditions.
2. Identify both positive or negative influences.
3. Define the obstacles and opportunities before you.

Some might compare the process to pain and pleasure – the pain of the current reality and the pleasure of your future reality. However we define it, we need to realize that we are in control. We are the creators of our current existence and the builders of our future. We are the developers of change. When we look at our life and our current conditions, it is easy to assign blame to others for putting you into this situation. But we need to realize that whether they put us there or not, we cannot change or control others. We can only change and control ourselves. Once we realize this, we can move forward with our life design much more easily and approach our choices with more freedom. So, let's begin to discover the things that stand in our way.

Wayne Dyer uses an excellent analogy in his book, *Excuses Begone!:*

> The past is a trail you leave behind, much like the wake of a speedboat. That is, it's a vanishing trail temporarily showing you where you were. The wake of the boat doesn't affect its course – obviously it can't, since it only appears behind the boat. So, consider this image when you exclaim that your past is the reason you aren't moving forward.

As a sailor, I can relate to this, although I remember a moment when the "past" seemed about ready to crash into the "present." It happened one Sunday afternoon as I was motoring up the channel between Sandusky Bay and the open waters of Lake Erie. My family and I were enjoying the ride and excited to set the sails as we reached the end of the channel. We were thrilled to embark upon a day of moderate breezes, sunshine and two- to three-foot waves. An excellent day for a light sail. As we were about midway through the channel, my niece looked back and gasped. "Uncle Dennis, look what's behind us." There it was, a massive ore boat bearing down on us about a hundred yards away. We knew the tanker would stay on course and we needed to move rather quickly – which we did! If your past makes you feel grief or guilt or self-pity, it can seem like a massive ore boat about to swamp you, and you may have to move fast to get out of its way.

Wayne Dyer is right when he says the past should only be a reference to our experiences, not an indicator about where we are going. It is up to us to free ourselves and limit the influence of our past. It's true that our experiences have created who we are, and we need to understand how they have impacted our lives and decisions. But these experiences are in our past, and we can only control what is in our future. So, let's get back to what we can control, look at our current reality and begin to work on the obstacles that stand in our way. It may be necessary to look back and reflect on our past for reference, but we can know that our future is ahead of us and is filled with vast possibilities.

The first thing any of us needs to decide is whether we are willing to change our life. This is so hard that it can be the most important obstacle. Often, we can recognize people, responsibilities, and routines as primary obstacles in our life, but we overlook our own resistance to change. However, if we make the commitment to change and are willing to proceed in making changes, very little will stand in our way. When we identify those people, relationships, responsibilities, tasks, and other obstacles, we will be able to begin to map out the process for making changes. We must get to a point where we can see our future clearly and how we are going to get past the hurdles impeding our progress.

It will help if you take some time to make out a detailed list of the changes that you need to make, tasks that you need to eliminate, people who are not reinforcing your dreams and routines that constantly steal time from your creative endeavors. For each obstacle you list, develop a plan for how to deal with it. There are different solutions for each one of these obstacles, and it does not mean that you have to eliminate a friendship or neglect a responsibility, but through modifying your commitments, reorganizing your time and, yes, maybe eliminating some activities, you will be able to reach that zero point where the pain ends or has been minimized and you are ready to dedicate your time to finding the pleasure of building a future filled with your most important dreams, freely, without the anchor of past responsibilities and fears. Ask the right questions and be realistic in your analysis of the problems. In the words of Ralph Waldo Emerson, "When we have arrived at the question, the answer is already near."

Bill Burnett and Dave Evans, in *Designing Your Life*, highly recommend finding the problems facing you. To them, problem-finding is as important as problem-solving. What you select as your most significant problems and which problems you decide to work on are critical decisions and will guide your search for your new directions in life. Take plenty of time to understand how you wish to react to the obstacles that are before you. Know where you want to head in life and come to grips with those things that keep you from getting there. Think clearly. Don't make excuses. Don't assign blame. You are the only one in control. Identify clearly what the problems are and approach their resolution with intelligence and optimism.

Optimism won't prevent negative events from happening; optimism will ensure that you respond to those negative events in the most beneficial way possible— a way that leads to positive outcomes.

—Darrin Donnelly

GET TO ZERO

Sense of agency refers to the individual's assumption of responsibility for the continuous journey to develop one's spirit. This requires people to accept their shortcomings and imperfections and to realize that they are the primary authors of their lives.

—Martin Seligman

As a designer, I like to make things simple and solve problems through the design process. I am a builder, a person who likes to start with a clean slate, imagine the future and develop the process that will help get you there. So, as I look at the problems facing so many of us, I find solutions by breaking problem-solving down into three phases.

DISCOVERY PHASE

First, we need to understand the problem. What is inhibiting us from reaching the next level in our lives? What stands in the way of achieving an exciting life – one that brings us pleasure on a daily basis. We need to face reality with clarity and determine the things, situations, and people in the way of achieving great accomplishments in our lives. We need to approach this analytically and identify what is in the way of our success. This is the discovery process.

We who are trying to better our lives and hoping to reach a state of well-being and life satisfaction need to do research to accurately analyze and diagnose the things we perceive as problems and through the discovery process, find answers. We all desire to achieve certain goals. We have plans for a day or a week and often cannot accomplish those plans because of outside circumstances in the way. We must identify those. Perhaps we can do this on our own. Perhaps we will need to get professional help to understand the reality of our situation. Either way, we need to come to grips with the truth. Making a list can help you identify those obstacles that stand in your way.

OBSTACLES TO PROGRESS

1. Who stands in the way of your reaching a life of well-being and satisfaction? (Remember to consider yourself as a person standing in your way.)
2. What responsibilities usurp your time from things you enjoy and know would help you achieve your true desires?
3. What distractions keep you from enjoying the process of working toward a happier and more productive life?
4. What outside factors dominate your life and keep you from enjoying your personal, professional, and spiritual life?

Develop these lists in much more detail, if you wish, and customize them to your situation. In the end what you need to do is to come to grips with your current reality, identify the problems and the people who are holding you back. Put them on a master list and begin to understand all the barriers in your journey for self-betterment.

THE ZERO POINT

Once you have identified everything to change, modify, or eliminate from your life, you can make out a clear, realistic list of obstacles you will need to deal with. If you think of your life as a chart filled with responsibilities and requirements, it becomes a complex reality. How can you deal with this? Let's start with reviewing that master list that you created in the discovery phase. Review each problem area. Next to each problem, write a possible solution or several solutions. It might be to eliminate the problem, change the problem or find a new way to integrate the problem into your new vision. Through this process, you reach a point where each problem has been identified and a resolution has been suggested. If you could erase each problem from the list, you would get to a zero point where there are no problems remaining. Each problem has a solution, and soon you will be working with a clean slate.

This may sound simple, but the problems you confront will take time to resolve. If you write them down on a master list and indicate possible solutions, you can see them with more clarity. Next, let's move these problems to another piece of paper and a new master list. What remains? Another blank sheet of paper, a symbol of opportunity. A blank sheet with no problems, no obstacles no one standing in the way. Now you have gotten to zero. And at this point you are ready to begin planning.

BUILDING A FUTURE

Now the excitement begins. Now you have nothing standing in your way. You have erased, solved, or managed the problems in your life, or at least relegated then to a worksheet. Now you are ready to unleash your imagination, identify your true dreams and start building the life you want. But this cannot be done until you have reached the zero point. If you keep your problems on the table, they continue to confuse the issue, get in the way of creative planning, and be an obstacle. Now, with the problems put aside, you can plan freely, envision your new life with all of the dreams and desires that you have always wanted. Build a new list or revisit your old list and revise it. Place every dream and desire on the new master list. You need to enjoy the process freely until everything that you want for your future is on the list.

You are the designer of your future. You are the author of your life. Let's fill our lists with words of excitement and enthusiasm and create a new life of meaning and personal fulfillment.

Your life is not a thing, it's an experience; the fun comes from designing and enjoying the experience.

—Bill Burnett

FIND FREEDOM

In my life, the only common factor in all my failed relationships is me. The common factor in all my struggles and setbacks that finite leaders face is their own finite thinking. To admit that takes courage. To work to open one's mind to a new worldview takes even more courage.

—Simon Sinek

Re-shaping your life is a process, one that begins with self-understanding. It is difficult to be creative when things are nagging you. Distractions. Annoyances. Obstacles. We need to come to grips with the things in the way of our creative potential. We need to find a place of freedom from the things on our mind, freedom from responsibilities. We need to reach a space where our mind is open and free to imagine and free to innovate. We need a *Tabula Rasa* – a clean slate. When you can identify the obstacles and lay out resolutions for each of them, you are now able to begin building a new life plan with revitalized inspiration.

There are two parts to the creative process for making changes in your life. One is discovery, which identifies the problems in your way. The second is building, during which you delineate your new vision. Taking care of the problems is just as important as dreaming about the future. You need to get to a point where your mind is free and clear, and you can think without restrictions. If you are constantly pulled back from your planning by the threats inherent in your current reality, you will not be able to accomplish your new vision. In the wonderful words of Martin Seligman, "Action is not driven by the past, but pulled by the future."

The conditions in your current reality can be extremely stressful and can leave you frozen in your tracks. Emily Fletcher, one of the great teachers and advocates of meditation in our country, instructs readers how to confront stressful events and reduce their negative impact. She says, "There is no such thing as a stressful situation, only stressful responses to a given situation. In other words, stress is not what happens to you; stress is your reaction to what happens to you." As you begin to understand the problems you face and the barriers to your preferred future, place them in proper perspective, understand their potential irrelevance and decrease your stressful response.

As you identify the major problems impeding your progress, you can approach each problem knowing there is a solution, whether it is to eliminate the problem, change its dynamics or re-imagine it. Sometimes you might even be able to turn a problem into an advantage. When this is accomplished for each difficulty you face, you can reach your point of freedom. Freedom to begin again. Freedom to look toward a new future without the anchors of the past. Freedom to let your untethered imagination explode with excitement and fill with creativity.

Practice back-from-the-future thinking. Project forward five years and then look back mentally to where you are today. Imagine the steps you would have had to take to make your future vision a reality. This exercise of projecting forward and then looking back to the present is extremely powerful in clarifying what you want and what you will have to do to achieve it.

—Brian Tracy

TACKLE YOUR PROBLEMS: TWELVE STEPS

1. What obstacles stand in your way?
2. Clearly state each problem.
3. Analyze the problem: Why is it a problem?
4. What conditions help make it a problem?
5. What people help make it a problem?
6. How does this problem make you feel?
7. Envision your life without the problem.
8. Imagine alternative realities without the problem.
9. Unleash your imagination to explore possible solutions.
10. Use research and discovery to support possible solutions.
11. Imagine a new reality that makes the problem obsolete.
12. Define and implement changes you might make to solve each problem, one by one.

TACKLE YOUR PROBLEMS WORKSHEET

To move forward, you must understand your current reality, see the obstacles in your way and change, modify or eliminate them. The following questions will help you identify many of the problem areas and find solutions.

List obstacles to achieving your goals.

1. _____

2. _____

3. _____

4. _____

5. _____

Which problems are most important?

1._____

2._____

3._____

4._____

5._____

How are these problems getting in the way of reaching your preferred future?

1._____

2._____

3._____

4._____

5._____

Who stands in your way or contributes to your problems?

1._____

2._____

3._____

4._____

5._____

List additional fears, barriers or other factors causing problems for you.

1._____

2._____

3._____

4._____

5._____

Are you causing some of the problems? How do you influence some of the problems?

1._____

2._____

3._____

4._____

5._____

Unleash your imagination to explore possible solutions to each major problem.

1._____

2._____

3._____

4._____

5._____

From the lists above, select the three most important problems you face and would like to eliminate. List them below and write an action statement about what to do to address the problem. Example: I want to be financially secure when I retire, so I will find a financial planner and begin discussions.

1. _____

_____

_____

2. _____

_____

_____

3. _____

_____

_____

s i x

UNLEASH YOUR CREATIVE SPIRIT

EMBRACE CREATIVITY

The common strands that seemed to transcend all creative fields was an openness to one's inner life, a preference for complexity and ambiguity, an unusually high tolerance for disorder and disarray, the ability to extract order from chaos, independence, unconventionality, and a willingness to take risks.

—Scott Barry Kaufman

CREATIVITY IS AT THE HEART of combining imagination with a spark of curiosity. Constantly asking questions, searching for the basis of our beliefs, and dreaming of the impossible are all parts of the pursuit of the creative experience. But creativity is a state of mind. Placing ourselves in a free space of open-mindedness, speculating without reservation or concern for "correctness" and living free to experiment are all enveloped in the creative atmosphere. It is a way of life, a license to approach our pursuits in a manner that hasn't been done before. Mike Vance writes, "Creativity is the making of the new and the rearranging of the old in a new way." With creativity, we can combine unrelated concepts in a new way or make changes to an existing concept to unearth a new functionality or new uses.

All possible ideas, dreams and hopes are inside us. We are unique individuals. No one is like us and consequently our own personality is, in fact, a creative entity. To quote Wayne Muller, "Our life is not a problem to be solved, it is a gift to be opened." Life as a gift is a wonderful expression. All the ideas we need, all the concepts, are already inside of us ready to be opened, nurtured and brought to reality. Everyone can use their creativity to expand their life, stretch their imagination and develop an exceptional life.

There are no formulas for creativity. But if we approach life with an open mind and a quest for new experiences, we give ourselves a chance to harness our creativity and take paths we have not walked before. Many think that creativity is something experienced only in the arts. True, creativity is imperative in the arts, whether in music, painting, architecture, literature, theater, or film. But creativity is not limited only to the arts. It can be a vital part of all professional activities. Solving problems is a creative act. Finding the most appropriate solutions to a business problem can require all our creativity. Analyzing a patient's symptoms in the medical field is an analytical process, but finding solutions for that patient's concerns will take creativity and imagination. Engineers, accountants, and many other professionals are problem-solvers who regularly need to use their creativity to think differently to develop the most effective solutions.

Being creative allows us to question life, to be curious, and to try avenues other than the traditional approaches. Being creative is a way of life. It means not following the leader, not following the rules. It means freeing our mind, unleashing our imagination, and allowing our dreams to surface and our vision for our life to have clarity. Clear yourself of the routines that govern your life and use your creativity to build a life that you deserve and a life that only you can imagine.

As you approach designing your new life, think creatively. What are the possibilities? What visions could be developed? We are the designers of our lives. We have unique opportunities to approach life design without the conflicts of external demands, unreasonable budgets or technical procedures limiting us. We are free to dream, free to imagine and free to create. This is how we should approach creativity. Be curious. Unleash your desires. And don't be limited by anything. Release all your preconceptions and think with a new, free vision – unrestricted. Re-create yourself.

We don't stop playing because we grow old; we grow old because we stop playing.

—George Bernard Shaw

CHANGE YOUR LIFE

In order to effect true positive change in your experience, you must disregard how things are – as well as how others are seeing you – and give more of your attention to the way you prefer things to be.

—Esther and Jerry Hicks

Major changes in life, often at key turning points, will happen, and we must be willing to adapt to these changes. Graduating from high school and leaving home for college, getting married, having your first child, changing careers, retiring, divorce or the death of someone close to us are among the turning points that inevitably bring about change. And with each of these events we will experience anxieties that reflect our unwillingness to change. But we need to remember Buckminster Fuller's attitude to change: "You never change things by fighting the existing reality. To change something, build a new model that makes the existing model obsolete." I could read this quotation every day for the rest of my life and never tire of exploring its meaning. As Fuller suggests, we need to create a new reality, a new vision that makes the old existing reality obsolete. We need to create a fantastic new reality, so exciting that there is no question that we want to go there, live in that new space, and experience a fresh new reality.

Let's examine just one of these change-making phases of life – retirement. People approaching their retirement may see a future with a follow-the-leader mentality, filled with traditional activities, mindless routine, and a life without commitments. It may even make them focus on the nearness of death. This is an almost inevitable worry as we age, but it can haunt life at any age. Long ago I read the memoir of a woman with cancer. She described how some of her friends had already written her off and didn't bother to visit. And some who did were awkward or embarrassed to be in the room with one so close to death. When she shared these experiences with an elderly nurse, the nurse scoffed. "You're alive until you're dead," she said. "That's the fact of the matter." She was right. There's no point in obsessing about death and every reason to use each day until then as well and as happily as we possibly can.

Among us are retirees who envision retirement as one of the most exciting phases in life. To me, retirement is not an end goal. It is a phase of life to fill with new opportunities and accomplishments. This takes imagination and planning but could hardly be more fulfilling. Our life expectancy has grown over our lifetime. When the first baby boomers were born, life expectancy in the U.S. was 64 for men, 69 for women. Now, a sixty-five-year-old man can expect to live 18 more years and a woman almost 21 more years. For many of us "retirement" has stretched out to be as long as our entire childhood and teenage years. It can give us another twenty-five or even thirty years of life after age 65. Today, there is no such thing as a traditional retirement. How have you planned for this? What are you going to do with this long, luxurious period of time?

Think of Thomas Moore's concept of "re-tire." It is particularly important to this concept of change. In other words, it is a time to put on new tires, recharge our batteries, tune up our engines and enter that next phase of life, which can be more exciting than anything that we have ever experienced before. Putting on new tires allows us to dream and use our imagination, unshackled by the restraints of our current professional career. It could free us to make a new contribution to our profession, our community, our country and to our world. What is also exciting about this new definition of retirement, is that it can happen any time in our career. Change is essential to a vibrant life. Why not re-tire in mid-career? Why not re-tire in our thirties or fifties? While we may have to continue bringing in wages or a salary at any life stage, "retirement" only means change, and if we can design our new life with excitement and optimism, re-tiring can be a rewarding adventure any time in our life.

Frank Lloyd Wright, the great American architect, continued to create until the last day of his life, when he was 92. His life pattern reminds us that we have precious gifts – our life, our body, our mind, and our talents, and we cannot waste them. The idea of "down time" is silly. Every day, every hour, every minute of our life is a gift given to us to help us make our contribution to our world. We can harness our experiences, our talents, our beliefs, and our knowledge to continue creating, continue contributing, and continue giving back every day of our lives. Frank Lloyd Wright, whose masterpiece, the Guggenheim Museum in New York City, opened six months after he died. All his life, he invested in beauty. What do you cherish? What do you want to invest in? How can you make your contribution to humanity throughout your life?

Your visions will become clear only when you can look into your own heart. Who looks outside, dreams; who looks inside, awakes.

—Carl Jung

BUILD A PRETEND WORLD

See yourself where you want to be and then be there. Don't be in the past. Be there! Act like the person you want to become.

—Bob Proctor

We each live in a world of our own choosing, a world whose pieces and parts we select. We design this world and build it to fit our needs, preferences, and desires. From childhood, we construct this world for ourselves. We live, work, and play at our best in this world, having designed it instinctively for our optimum life. Some call it designing a life or building a dream castle or entering into a world of imagination. To me, it is the world as we pretend it to be, and as such, it has its own reality. We can build a pretend world, choose its parameters, define its rules, fill it with possibilities and live exciting lives within the world as we imagine it.

Like so many people, I am always thrilled to attend a Broadway musical and allow myself to slip into the playwright's imaginary world. The actors take us to another place, another environment, and another way of thinking about life. We are captured by that moment as we see the scenes, hear the dialogue and music, and see the acting and choreography. A playwright creates a pretend world, and we willingly suspend disbelief in our desire to accept and experience the playwright's world. The playwright gives us the key to this invented world and allows us to believe that we are really there.

Some have said that seeing is believing, but I think the opposite is even more important: believing is seeing. That is the truth in the saying, "When the student is ready, the teacher will appear." When we believe, we can see. Through belief, we create a vision of our own. If we believe with enough conviction, life has no barriers but is filled with possibilities.

Living in a world of our own construct stimulates our imagination and connects us to creativity. The outside world is distracting, filled with a multitude of negative forces all too ready to steal away our optimism and hopefulness. But we, who are required to make many choices in life, can choose what to read, what to remember, what to listen to, what to watch, who to talk with and who to believe. We must choose wisely and selectively to reinforce the world as we choose it to be. We each live in a world we have built for ourselves. It is what makes us all individuals, what defines who we are and what we believe.

But most importantly, living in a world of our own allows us to control the landscape of our lives, see the horizon and live in hope. The sun can always shine in your life if you live in a world of your own design. You can always approach life optimistically if the world as you envision it is designed to unveil the most positive aspects of your thinking. In such a space of our own making, we can cast aside all the negative forces that constantly seek to impinge upon us. And why not be in such a space?

It can be a beautiful place, a world of possibilities, a world with an exciting vision. The best families are those under the umbrella of a parent or grandparent whose vision is a family governed by mutual support and kindness, encircled in hope and love. The strongest individuals live in a magical world that unleashes all the forces of inspiration and encourages the daily rediscovery of joy and possibility.

Is this a world of make believe? One might say so, but what a wonderful phrase – "make believe": Make. Believe. We create, we build, we make what we believe in. We select all the most important values, ideas, wishes and beliefs and place them into our world – our pretend world. This is good. This is building a perfect life according to you and who you are. This is creating your vision and finding peace within your own mind, your own actions and within your own soul.

Pretend, dream, make believe and build the extraordinary life that is yours to have. Walk around the roadblocks of negativity, egotism, and self-pity. Or bound over them! Reject any negative forces threatening to keep you from realizing your vision. Unleash the possibilities within yourself. Build your optimum life by unleashing your imagination and letting your make-believe world reinforce your sense of hope and create the life you choose. After all, it is your life. You are its designer and the one who builds your belief system. You are the playwright of your life.

But maybe happiness isn't in the choosing. Maybe it's in the fiction, in the pretending: that wherever we have ended up is where we intended to be all along.

—Lauren Oliver

REINVENT YOURSELF

We are always growing from the present into the future, and therefore always changing. With each change comes a new design. Life is not an outcome; it's more like a dance. Life design is just a really good set of dance moves. Life is never done (until it is), and life design is never done (until you're done).

—Bill Burnett and Dave Evans

Do you need to reinvent your life? Reinvention is one of the last phases of making changes to your life that address the kind of problems and concerns that keep you awake at night. The process of change follows the sequence in this thought:

> If you can dream it, you can believe it, and
> if you can believe it, you can see it, and
> if you can see it, you can achieve it.

To achieve anything, you need to believe in it and be reinforced by that belief enough to keep you excited about achieving it. To achieve your new life vision, you need to reinvent your life from here on and into the future.

Burnett and Evans see life as a dance. To me, life is like a symphony, a beautifully written musical score driven by a singular concept and filled with variations and intrigue. The symphony is an invention. It is a musical story filled with emotions and enhanced by the dynamics of a multitude of notes, chords, and timing. It is a complex integration of ideas, sequences, and movements, well designed, mathematically synchronized, and leading to a planned climax.

Through the process of re-invention in our lives, we create a new direction that will reinforce our desires and dreams. To invent is to create something that has never been done before. The process involves collecting all our experiences, knowledge, hopes and dreams and integrating them into a perfect direction for our life as we develop its next phase. I say, 'next phase,' because if done properly, reinvention will bring us to a new phase that casts aside all those negative forces that make our life less than perfect and allows our aspirations to bloom. We are always moving toward a next phase in our lives. How important each phase is, is up to you to decide.

Re-invention requires us to confront the fears, anxieties and external forces affecting our current life. It involves facing those threats and throwing out or fixing what needs to be discarded or resolved. Once we eliminate the problems that annoy us, we can approach our reinvention with a clean slate. It's like beginning a painting on a fresh, new canvas – nothing but possibilities, nothing but creative freedom. And the results will be our own masterpiece, a life filled with thrilling anticipation and excitement. In the words of Malcolm Gladwell, "Innovators have to be open. They have to be able to imagine things that others cannot and be willing to challenge their own preconceptions."

Our main design project in life is to design our own life – a wonderful opportunity. Why not approach it with excitement and optimism? By harnessing our knowledge and experience, we can make significant and creative contributions to our family, profession, community, and world. This is not only an opportunity, but also our responsibility: giving back does not stop until our last day on this earth. How exciting is that?

People who are crazy enough to think they can change the world are the only ones who do.

—Gary Keller

BELIEVE IN YOURSELF

Your dominant thoughts always match your manifestations, and so, once you understand the absolute correlations between your thoughts, how you feel, and what is manifesting in your experience, you can then accurately predict everything that will come into your life.

—Esther and Jerry Hicks

One of the most fascinating books that I have read recently is *The Law of Attraction*. The authors, Esther and Jerry Hicks, argue that we are in total control of our lives. They believe that what we think and feel has everything to do with what we can expect to occur in our lives. In a sense, it's a radical idea. Can our beliefs actually change our future? Of course they can! Every positive change we make in our lives begins with believing we can do it.

- Is joy something that you want to bring onto your life? If that is true, then how do you achieve it?
- If happiness is something that you want as part of your life? Then how do you achieve it?
- If friendships are something that you want to nourish and bring to your life, how is this done?

According to *The Law of Attraction,* we manifest what we are thinking, what we are feeling and what we believe. If we want to attract people into our life who are positive and happy, we need first to be positive and happy. We attract what we are feeling. If we want to attract more interesting people, first be a more interesting person. We attract what we are feeling. If we want to attract more joy into our life, we need to be more joyous ourselves. We attract what we are feeling. We attract what we believe. What we think is what will manifest itself in our life.

So, to develop a plan for our life, filled with the feelings and experiences we wish to have, we must possess those feelings as we develop the plan and execute the plan. We attract who we are. We attract how we are feeling. We attract into our life the experiences and people who share our beliefs. This concept works through a logical series of steps. First, we need to desire something so powerfully that it becomes a guiding force in our life, almost an obsession. When our subconscious resonates with this desire, everything we see and experience connects with this desire. When we are ready to say yes to our dreams and desires, the avenues for acquiring them become more obvious. The paths to acquiring our desires have always been there, but when we dedicate ourselves to these desires, they manifest themselves and become more obvious. This is the process of editing and selecting what influences us, what becomes important to us and what we choose to see.

When your beliefs and desires are powerful, they will influence what you see, hear, and feel. You will begin to see things you may never have noticed before and to favor some of the images in front of you. They may have always been there, but when you see with new eyes, from a new point of view and with new intentions, you can expect your desires and dreams to enter your life.

When you make choices that expedite the manifestation of your dreams, you are in control. When you begin to visualize the realization of your dreams, you will begin to see pathways for achieving them. If you believe deeply that your dreams and desires are achievable, you will make opportunities happen. You will make choices in your life that hasten your search, and through this selection process you will be guided to your destination, and your dreams will be realized. Thich Nhat Hanh writes:

> Our mind is like a garden in which there are all kinds of seeds; seeds of joy, peace, mindfulness, understanding and love, but also seeds of craving, anger, fear, hate, and forgetfulness. How you act and the quality of your life depends on which seeds you water… If you water a seed of peace in your mind, peace will grow. When the seed of happiness in you is watered, your happiness will bloom.

Believe in yourself. Believe in your potential. Be optimistic, and let your feelings and thoughts attract the people and experiences you want to have. As LL Cool J says, you need to "maximize your potential." You will never be satisfied in just reaching your goal, because once you reach it, you will set higher goals. This is a continuous process of growth. The more you grow, the more you will see, and the larger the world will become. This will give your dreams more and more room to expand. Does this work? Yes, but only if you believe it will.

NOURISH HOPE

You are not here merely to make a living, you are here in order to enable the world to live more amply, with greater vision, with a finer spirit of hope and achievement. You are here to enrich the world, and you impoverish yourself if you forget the errand.

—Woodrow Wilson

When I begin to write today, I am sitting at my computer as the Covid-19 makes its attack on the United States. When Woodrow Wilson said, *"You are here to enrich the world, and you impoverish yourself if you forget the errand,"* the United States was in the midst of the last pandemic, the 1917-1918 flu. Both pandemics had or are having a devastating effect on all the countries of the world, on the families who have experienced loss, on businesses who have had to close, and on economies everywhere. It is changing our way of life.

- What will the future hold?
- How will life look on the other side of this crisis?
- How do we wrestle with the idea of hope for the future?

These complex issues may cause us to question the very idea of hope. Is hope a realistic wish? Is it just a wonderful dream? Or can it be ignited to provide, once again, a potential of growth achieved and dreams realized? Does hope still have a place in our existence?

Hope is nothing more than the realization that the future can be better; things can improve; conditions will inevitably change, and we can use that change to realize our dreams and aspirations. But we live in the now. We have control only over what we do now, not in the past nor in the future. In the future lies our hope for an improved life, better conditions, and the potential for attracting those things that will bring us pleasure, reinforce our happiness, and help us achieve our goals. We are all driven by the concept of hope. It is what makes us think and plan with the anticipation of an improved quality of life. Without hope, there is only the current reality without the potential for change and without the life improvements that an innovative mind can offer. We all live in a set of circumstances that restrict us, where obstacles stand in the way of our progress. And we hope that we can alter these conditions so that we can advance into a new reality, one that reinforces our dreams and desires.

We need to look at hope in a way that does not become discouraging. First, hope is the anticipation of a reinvented and revitalized future. A future that allows us to improve our current condition. However, hope is not enough. First, your desired future does not come by accident. You must work toward achieving it. Second, there are potential obstacles in your way. And third, anticipating your future has the potential for creating anxiety, because we know our pursuit may fail. You may not reach your goals. The fear of failure can be strong enough to deter us from even trying, but where's the sense in that? We should adapt the old saying about love: "Better to have tried and failed than never to have tried at all." There's no shame in failure. And in all of this, hope is essential. Those who succeed in life and in business are optimistic and excited about their future potential. They want their dreams to be realized, and they can live with the risk of failure.

We all find excitement in stretching our current abilities and reaching to set our goals higher than we thought possible. I am struck by this quote by Ellen Johnson Sirleaf. "The size of your dreams must always exceed your current capacity to achieve them. If your dreams do not scare you, they are not big enough." This is exciting. This is enough to inspire hope. And in the words of Michelangelo, "The greater danger for most of us is not that our aim is too high and we miss it, but that it is too low and we reach it." We are driven to exceed. And this is supported by optimism and tells us that hope is real. There is a light at the end; change cannot be stopped, but we can shape our future. The question to me is, how can we influence change, nourish its positive outcomes, and build our future according to our guidelines.

Wayne Dyer says, "The danger is not in false hope, rather it is in no hope or low hope, and consequently our objectives and aims are diminished by our beliefs before they can be worked on and materialized." Dyer's many exceptional philosophies give us the impetus for excelling in our expectations and placing trust in hope. As we create our future, we must approach it with the belief that our achievements are possible. The more you invest in developing your personal plan for the future, the more you come to believe in the possibility that it will materialize. Hope is essential to motivating us to excel and to reach higher than we think we can. It is what drives us to manifest our dreams and to design the pathways to achievement.

The future is not some place we are going to, but one we are creating. The paths are not to be found, but made, and the activity of making them, changes both the maker and the destination.

—M. J. Ryan

LEARN BY EXPERIMENTING

Change can often be difficult, and it will probably seem easier to just stick with what you are already doing. That thinking can be dangerous. You're only kicking the can down the road, and you risk waking up one day, years later, looking into the mirror, asking yourself: 'What am I doing with my life?'

—Clayton Christensen

Our lives are an experiment. Every day is a new day with new challenges and encounters that affect our thinking and our decisions. Every time we enter into a new problem resolution, it becomes an experiment. What model should we follow to analyze the problem? What data should we use to help to evaluate the circumstances? All these factors will be done with logic and a past history but will be done as an experiment. Initial results might fail, but with the knowledge we gain, we move on to try again. Every creative design project is an experiment. There are always many solutions to solving a problem. There are always many approaches to a solution and with our experience on similar and previous projects, we start with the best practices, knowing how they worked in the past. But each problem is a new problem, and the process is still experimental.

As Covid-19 raged throughout the world, scientists experimented to find a vaccine and to find an antibody that would help reduce the severity of the virus. Is there a sure path to finding these? No. That's why scientists were experimenting, using the best of their knowledge and experience to apply the most appropriate approach in their research. Finding cures for all types of disease continues throughout the world.

Some will be resolved. Many will be on-going. Experimentation is not a negative word. It is used every day in scientific research, within the design professions, in medicine, engineering and any field charged with finding answers to problems. In the same way, our lives are an experiment.

The most difficult part of planning our lives is that we have choices. Although Achor says, "the more interpretations of the world you can see, the better you can construct the prism of success," sometimes it seems like we have too many choices. In fact, we have all the choices in the world. As we open our mind to the possibilities, we can see that we are not limited in choices and that becomes a problem. In *Designing Your Life,* Burnett and Evans suggest that life offers each of us many possible paths.

We can decide what kind of life we choose to live. Trying several choices shows how the whole business of life is an experiment. Burnett and Evans even suggest that we never finish designing our lives. They say, "You aren't designing the rest of your life; you are designing what's next." This is a remarkable insight. Many people feel like they must make lifelong decisions without realizing that the conditions in their lives change and with that their plans must be flexible and adapt to changing circumstances. Life planning is an experiment. We take it one step at a time with what we know now. Tomorrow, next month or next year will bring changing criteria, as 9/11 or the 2020 pandemic reminded us so forcefully. All such changes will need to be brought into the life equation, and we will need to experiment once again.

We can make major conceptual decisions about our life and make changes that will improve our daily life both now and into the future. We have many possible lives that we could lead. Experiment with them and choose the one that is the most exciting, most rewarding and is the best fit for you – at this time. Don't be afraid to experiment. As we strive for answers to our questions and try to find solutions to the problems we face, many of our experiments will not solve the problem, but that is all part of the process of finding the best answers – the best solutions. You will have failures as you try to find solutions in your life planning. This should not be discouraging. Failures just notify you that you are getting closer to the real solution. A friend of mine who is a top salesperson explained the success he achieved in his earliest days like this:

> I was assigned to make cold calls, and while most people hate these, I had been told that about one in ten would be successful. So, as I called, I counted, and the closer I got to the tenth call the more excited I got. Success was right around the corner!

I have no doubt that his confidence and excitement contributed greatly to his success, even though his statistics were probably wrong. Nevertheless, just when his competitors were being beaten down by 'failure,' he was revving up for the breakthrough he was sure was coming. As you experiment, expect failure, and know that every failure gives you the opportunity to learn, evaluate and try again. Each failure puts you closer to success. Brian Tracy reminds us of the need to take action:

> You don't wait for good things to happen to you. You go out and make things happen…. Life is very much like a buffet line. Life is self-serve. Nobody brings it to you. You have to get up, accept responsibility and serve yourself.

We are responsible for our own lives, but there is often no one clear path set out for us as we begin our journey. It is essential to experiment with all sorts of possibilities for the broader concepts as well as the finite details of our lives. But we need to approach these decisions with excitement knowing the end results will bring new opportunities and new horizons to our lives. Some of the decisions we make will surely fail, and our experiments will take us in unexpected directions, including some that will need to be corrected when we find that they are going off to nowhere. But these are all our decisions, and we have the right and responsibility to make changes. Experimenting is an exciting process, and it will open doors you never knew existed. Enjoy the process.

EXPERIENCE ENLIGHTENMENT

He who knows others is wise. He who knows himself is enlightened.

—Lao-Tzu

You open your eyes, the fog begins to lift, a clarity begins to emerge, and suddenly the brightness of the sun floods your view with brilliance, and everything becomes understood. That is enlightenment. It's the ah-ha moment. It's the time when answers come flowing and questions that have been on your mind forever are finally answered and the paths to finding solutions are realized.

Enlightenment can arrive at almost any moment in life. It can happen at the end of a long research study or when you finish reading a remarkable book. It can happen at major turning points in your life or merely after a session of meditation.

Think about the three phases of life – the learning phase, the production phase, and the enlightenment phase. Typically, the learning phase takes place between the ages of birth and one's final stage of formal education, but certainly can carry on into the early years of employment. These are the years of learning, forming understandings, developing concepts, and memorizing the facts and details of your chosen profession. As an adult, the first few years involve learning procedures, understanding the group with which you work and finding out how to fit into its long-term goals. It includes experiencing the danger zones and seeing opportunities that will allow you to make an impact.

After you have settled into the routines of adult life, you begin the second phase – the production phase. This is a phase for achievement. It includes making your contribution to your family, your employer, and your profession. In the production phase, you learn how to become a financial asset to yourself, your family, and your company. The learning process continues, but at this point you have adapted, learned the basics, understood the organization's goals and are in full production.

The last phase, the enlightenment phase, may enter at the later stages of your career. It is when all your learning, experience and understanding become integrated to allow you to see the bigger picture of your life. The "whys" are answered. The meanings are clarified. And your mission is understood. It is when you can see your life from the 30,000 feet level and can grasp an enlightened understanding of how it all works. This is an exciting phase of life. You can enter it with confidence, with knowledge and with authority. You have run the race, have seen the pitfalls, and have survived. Whether enlightenment arrives near the end of your life, at mid-career or during the beginning years, it is a time when your senses are heightened so you can see the relevance in all your decisions and actions. Your life becomes a synthesis of your learning, experience, dreams, ambitions, and aspirations, and all can be seen with a greater and more connected meaning.

The more we can open our minds, the sooner enlightenment will arrive. Being able to see everything with authenticity, honesty and clarity is essential to being in a state of enlightenment. All the experience we gain throughout our life will have significance if it is filtered through an open mind. We need to free our mind of egotism, clutter, and pre-suppositions and look for the truth. We need to ask what is real and see how it can bring meaning to our life. Enlightenment is a special time in our life when all of our knowledge, concerns, worries and visions of the future come together and, as though we tried on a new pair of glasses, we can see more clearly, with new understanding and enthusiasm.

When will enlightenment become present in your life? To become enlightened, you must make an attempt to know yourself and understand the relevance of the experiences you have had throughout your life, have an open mind, and pursue a search for meaning. Don't force it. All of a sudden, it will happen – a realization that brings together many different ideas or thoughts or an insight that summarizes concepts you have been working on. Most importantly, keep learning, keep searching, and keep your mind open to new realities, new visions, and new ways of thinking differently, ways that ignite insights important to you. You will only find what you are looking for.

Everyone can achieve something significant. The key is not effort, but finding the right thing to achieve.

—Richard Koch

seven

UNLEASH YOUR NEW VISION

THINK ABOUT REINCARNATION / TRANSMIGRATION

A large proportion of human suffering occurs because people think they only live once. When they become fully aware that the present life is only one point in the eternal flow of time, and that they have lived in the past and will live again in the future, they will understand that their future lives will depend on their present life and also that they can choose what kind of life they will live in the future.

—The Essence of Buddha

BELIEF IN THE AFTERLIFE is one of the most important elements in most, if not all, religions. It gives believers hope that their life will not end with their death, but that an afterlife exists in some form, in some other place. The soul, or whatever the religion considers the basis of existence, continues on in another form to live once again. The details of the belief – whether one believes their soul will live on in heaven, or on another galaxy or here on Earth – is part of what differentiates the various religions.

Reincarnation is a central belief in Indian religions, including Jainism, Buddhism, Sikhism and Hinduism, which finds its origins in ancient Greek philosophers such as Pythagoras, Plato, and Socrates. Another term for reincarnation is transmigration, or the migration from one life to another life. The afterlife may take on many forms and definitions, but in most instances involves the transition from one's current body to another form. This is what instills hope in believers – that while this life may be over in its current form, there is another waiting for us to discover.

Whether this transition is called reincarnation or heaven, I find the concept fascinating because it is analogous to the transition we make through self-actualization. Those who believe in a traditional reincarnation or afterlife must wait until their death. But I would ask, why wait? Why wait when you can make the transition now? I don't mean to choose death, but rather, to make that transition to another life while still living. Now. Choose the elements of a perfect life right now, right here in your current form. If you are wanting change in your life, if you envision a more ideal future, why not reincarnate yourself in this current life? What a tremendous opportunity that would be. And you can do it. I have been talking about change and the benefit of embracing change rather than resisting it. You can make the decisions that will improve your life and implement changes that will create the life you prefer – a perfect life with all the elements that you choose. You can "reincarnate" right now in this life.

Let's speculate for a moment. In your reincarnation, who would you prefer to be, what personality would you like to emulate? Think of all the people you admire – perhaps mentors who have provided guidance. I might choose Frank Lloyd Wright, or perhaps Thomas Jefferson or maybe Pablo Picasso. Being great designers and artists, they would certainly offer tremendous guidance in forming my reincarnated life. Next, think of where you would like to live in the world. Would it be in the United States, and if so, what part of the country? What would you like to be doing? What would your professional interests be, and what type of work would you like to do? Would it be designing significant buildings, painting beautiful images on canvas, or perhaps, working on major scientific research? In your new life, who would be your friends and associates? Would they be people you know or people you have heard about and would like to meet and befriend? How would you like to spend your leisure time? You might like to check your lists of places to visit, events to participate in and achievements that you would like to accomplish. You might want to harness your current interests or talents to pursue the activities, events, and places of interest to you and begin to place them into your planning process. Now, this is starting to get exciting.

What kind of home would you like to live in? Would it be a modest residence in the country with lots of acreage for raising animals and riding horses, or would it be a magnificent home on a hillside near the ocean with spectacular views of sailing ships and marine life? Or perhaps your desire would be to live in a large, bustling city where culture and the arts abound, and you could be a part of that experience every day. When I was making my decisions for my career, I knew that I always wanted to live in a university environment and be influenced by the fresh ideas of young students and to pursue learning, contribute to the cultural environment and advance my field of study. If you are a history enthusiast, you might choose to live in Great Britain, France, or Italy or maybe all three – one after the other. What a wonderful opportunity, to be able to make all these choices. You might say that this is pie-in-the-sky thinking. You might say it is daydreaming. It sure is! But this is what unleashing and stretching your imagination is all about – dreaming of the possibilities and then creating the plans to make them happen.

So, can reincarnation happen now? I think it can, at least in some sense, and I think you have the power to open that door and make your perfect life right here, right now. We don't know what the future holds for us, but we do know that we are here in the present and that it is our responsibility to make this present moment the most exciting, most challenging, and most rewarding experience possible. Enjoy the process, enjoy the dream, believe in the process of rebirth, transmigration, and reincarnation. But don't wait for it to happen later. Make it happen in your current life. It may take a little time to put all your desires and dreams in place, but with enthusiasm and a belief in your future, you can make it happen. Enjoy the process.

Renew, release, let go. Yesterday's gone. There's nothing you can do to bring it back. You can't 'should've' done something. You can only DO something. Renew yourself. Release that attachment. Today is a new day.

—Steve Maraboli

ASPIRE TO SIGNIFICANCE

Live in your imagination. Give yourself the freedom to wander into unfamiliar territory in your mind and to explore new possibilities in your fantasies, excluding nothing. These imaginative meanderings will ultimately become the catalysts for living an unlimited life.

—Wayne Dyer

After becoming more aware of your desires and dreams and attempting to connect those to your societal, professional, and family responsibilities, your next step is to focus your attention on formulating plans to convert your dreams and desires to action. In order to change, we must dig deep into our mind and our subconscious to allow our true desires to surface. But desires and dreams are one thing and achieving them is another. Eventually, you will need to select your most important objectives and focus on creating a plan to reach your primary ambitions and aspirations.

In 2019 I was invited to be on the faculty of the Keith Krach Transformational Leadership Workshop for college students. It was held at Bowling Green University, where about two thousand student leaders from around the country gathered for a one-week workshop on principle-centered leadership. I began my first class by asking each of the students to talk a little about themselves, identify their major and list a few of their goals in life. As I went around the room, they responded in typical ways, but one student surprised us all. He introduced himself by saying he was a political science major and that he intended to become president of the United States. Now that is an aspiration. That is a significant goal. I don't know if he will make it to the top, but with that kind of goal, he can't help but have an exciting life in his quest for achievement.

For each of us, the process of change might involve different priorities and will likely evolve as we embark on a sequence of action steps. Whatever your objective, you need to use a process that works successfully. The lists you have been developing should give you answers to the following questions, which are a good place to begin:

- What do you dream about doing, seeing, or accomplishing?
- Which of your desires and dreams are most important to you?
- Where do ambitions and aspirations fit into your self-discovery?

Next, think about how motivated you are to making change.

- How do you feel about your current reality?
- Why is achieving your dreams important to you?
- What problems or obstacles stand in the way?
- How easy or difficult will it be to manage these obstacles?

The answers to these questions are essential to manifesting your happiness and well-being. You can bring things together by answering these questions:

- How do your dreams and desires connect with your purpose in life?
- Can these high-priority dreams be directly tied to your mission and goals?

Using the following steps will provide a process for moving from dreams and aspirations to achievements. The process is a logical hierarchy of decision-making and actions to be taken.

1. Select your most important dreams and desires.
2. Connect your dreams and desires with your life's purpose.
3. Decide on your most important ambitions and aspirations.
4. Set goals for achieving your ambitions and aspirations.

5. Develop an action plan for achieving your goals.
6. Begin implementing the action plans for achieving your goals.

Aspirations are the overriding, lofty goals that surface after you have spent significant time understanding yourself and your purpose in life. They may be the most important part of manifesting your ambitions. When you aspire to achieving specific goals, you have become committed to a dream – a dream of significance to you. It could be a commitment to a cause, an ideal, or a philanthropic partnership. It could be a commitment to self-improvement, a research project or advancing to a leadership role in your profession. Usually, one aspires to goals of significance that will have a dramatic impact on family, society, profession, or a chosen cause. Understanding and focusing on beliefs, values, principles, and purpose will help influence and form aspirational goals.

Michelangelo lived to be 89, many decades longer than his peers. He was one of the greatest artists of all time. Wayne Dyer paraphrases one of Michelangelo's sayings about being aspirational this way: "Aim big, refuse to choose small thinking and low expectations, and above all, do not be seduced by the absurd idea that there is danger in having too much hope." Michelangelo and Dyer remind us not to stop at the dreaming phase or the imagination phase but to turn a fuzzy dream into a specific aspiration, an objective. By acknowledging and integrating your most important personal characteristics, you will discover how you can form a direction for your ambitions and change the world or, at least, change your life. It only takes one person to launch a campaign for a cause that could have a significant impact on improving the lives of people or making a major scientific discovery. Each of us can aspire to leading a life of significance.

What do you love? You gain courage from what you love. When you know where your treasure lies, when you know what is, for you, sacred and right, then you are filled with a clarity of purpose and a breathtaking capacity to act on what you believe.

—Wayne Muller

IDENTIFY YOUR FOREMOST DREAMS

Your desires reflect what's truest about you. If your current reality is nowhere close to the life you want, dreams are the fuel that will move you forward. If you want to access your full range of power, then commit to dreaming about your ideal life.

—Danielle LaPorte

It's exciting to build your vision by introducing your most important dreams to it. As you work toward building your new vision, include as many of the dreams you identified in the first chapter of this book as you can. And just as you have done in similar exercises, prioritize your list of dreams and desires so the foremost dreams will come to the top of the list. For seven years, I studied with business and life planning coach Richard Zalack. I remember one of his favorite sayings, which was, "You can have anything you want in life, but not everything." To this day, his idea has helped guide me through many decisions. As you enjoy the process of evaluating your dreams and highlighting your hopes for the future, you will build a list of your most important dreams and then incorporate them into your new life vision. It's your choice.

At this point in your life design, I want you to think freely and openly as though there were no obstacles in your way. Plan as though there were no problems to sidestep or people who have become distractions. We will deal with these in the next section. This is the time to review all the thinking that you have done so far. You have already listed your values, beliefs, dreams, desires, ambitions, aspirations, and purpose in life. All these elements are part of a puzzle that represents components of your new life, and your mission is to see how all of these parts and pieces will fit together to create a plan for an exceptional life.

Each plan will be different. Everyone's plan is based on their own research and discovery. You have already made wonderful observations in the discovery process, and your vision should reflect the uniqueness of your preferences and decisions. Being uninhibited in the selection process will allow you to select directions that are unrestricted. I don't mean to be unrealistic by taking you down this path. There is time to pull in the reins. But in the meantime, enjoy the process of allowing important dreams to emerge as you plan the details and pathways to your new adventure.

Keep in mind, that listing your foremost dreams and desires is not just a bucket list. Because, as you have learned, your desires may be much more than new things to buy or places to visit. Your list of desires should begin with how you want to feel. Doing something that makes you feel important, feel at peace, or feel a sense of joy is perhaps more important than the activity you are engaged in. Also, outside the typical bucket list are the things you want to achieve. Your dreams may involve making specific achievements in your education, your career, or your legacy. Achievements may lead to happiness and joy. And finally, your desired dreams, feelings, and achievements need to be connected to your life's purpose. To manifest total happiness and joy, each of these elements must be synchronized.

When you list your dreams and desires, you are on the path to achieving them. They become imbedded in your subconscious and are with you whether you are casually thinking about them, performing other tasks, or working directly toward achieving one of them. With this influence, you will be able to see new possibilities as they appear and take advantage of opportunities as they present themselves.

As you have read this book, you have become more aware of your preferences, and you have discovered what makes you happy and excited. You also have identified what you really love and are passionate about. Don't be practical at this point while you list the dreams that you wish to manifest in your future vision. There is always time for practicality. Think about your ideal life and select the most exciting elements to be a part of your new plan. As you go through this process, you will build a list of all the essential components of your preferred future. The most important ones will rise to the top of the list and will be a great guide for developing the structure of your new life vision.

What are your fantasies? What emerges in your daydreams? What creates a thrilling experience for you? These are the things that will help you choose the lists of dreams and desires that you have compiled. Don't be modest in your requests. Don't be conservative in your approach to the planning process. This is your dream. You only have one life. Make it a wonderful experience. When you have made a commitment to your vision, nothing will stand in the way of your success.

Life is what we make it. No one else can do it for you; no one has the right to tell us what it ought to be. We make our own goals. We define our own success. We don't get to choose where we start in life; we do get to choose the kind of people we become"

—Peter Buffet

RESOLVE PROBLEMS

In design thinking, we put as much emphasis on problem finding as we do on problem solving.... Deciding which problems to work on may be one of the most important decisions you make, because people can lose years (or a lifetime) working on the wrong problem.

—Bill Burnett

In *Designing Your Life*, Bill Burnett and Dave Evans highlight one of the issues that inhibits a person from freely redesigning their life – finding their real problems. It can be easy to dream about your future, wish for an ideal life and proceed happily to hope for a beautiful outcome. But, if there are problems in your way, you might only reach part of your vision and constantly be anchored to obstacles that diminish your chances of success. So, first let's find out what the real problems are that affect your happiness and your chances of achieving success in your search for change.

In a previous section, "Discover the Problems," I asked you to create a list of the problems you face and the negative influences that impede your ability to make progress toward achieving your goals. Even if these problems are real, they only get in your way when you let them. You choose the way you feel and the way you react to these problems. However, there are problems you face that even your most optimistic and positive spirit will find difficult to overcome. That is why you need to separate the problems into categories and tackle each on different fronts. There are problems you can solve, problems you can modify, problems you cannot solve but you can ignore, accept or in some other way ameliorate.

Let's look at problems from two points of view. First, there are external problems created by outside sources, like other people. These can be physical, work-related, with family or friends, or financial. Second, there are internal problems, ones that are in your mind, imbedded in your personality, and while these may seem more difficult to identify and control, they are the ones most in your control. Internal problems can be more significant than the external ones because they are deeply embedded in your attitudes, personality, and belief system. It could be difficult to see yourself as the problem and to realize that you are inhibiting resolutions to your problems. Denial and resistance can delay or prevent your ability to see or solve internal problems. It may help to sort problems into two categories:

EXTERNAL PROBLEMS

1. Problems relating to friends.
2. Problems relating to family.
3. Problems relating to your job.
4. Problems relating to your finances.
5. Problems relating to health and fitness.
6. Problems relating to your social life.
7. Problems relating to your spiritual convictions.

INTERNAL PROBLEMS

1. Problems relating to your preconceptions.
2. Problems relating to your perceptions.

3. Problems relating to your attitude.
4. Problems relating to your education.
5. Problems relating to your skills and abilities.
6. Problems relating to your relationships with people.
7. Problems relating to your health and fitness.
8. Problems relating to self-pity or excuses.
9. Problems relating to what you allow to influence your thinking.

These offer just a start at categorizing problems as internal or external. It is important to determine where the problems come from, whether they are from external sources that are difficult or impossible to control or internal sources. As you look at the problems listed in each of these categories, begin to understand the source of the problems and how they can be solved. Go back through your list of problems and tag each one: Fix/Eliminate, Modify/Improve, or Accept/Ignore. Giving your problems these tags will let you see which ones to work on and which to accept or ignore. Remember, you get to make the choice whether you allow the problem to be a problem or to actively try to find a solution. It's possible that a problem cannot be fixed. In this case you might need to just walk away. It may be a work-related situation, a family-related problem, an individual who constantly brings anxiety into your life, or an insecurity, self-destructive habit, or obsession. Friendships may need to be restructured, a new job may be in your future, and a family issue may need to be overlooked or adjusted to. People can be a major source of problems. Shawn Achor says in *Big Potential*, "The height of your potential is predicated by the people who surround you. So the key to creating a super bounce for your potential is to surround yourself with people who will lift you up rather than drag you down."

EXTERNAL PROBLEMS

1. Fix the problem so that it is no longer a problem.
2. Modify the problem so it can be tolerated.
3. Ignore the problem.

4. Give the problem to someone else.
5. Wait until the problem goes away by itself.
6. See the problem from a different point of view.
7. See if you can reframe the problem and convert it to an opportunity.
8. Create new ways to solve the problem.

INTERNAL PROBLEMS

1. Change your attitude about the problem.
2. Change your perception of the problem.
3. Determine why you feel the way you do about the problem.
4. Determine why it is a problem.
5. Develop a positive attitude.
6. Determine how you could live with the problem.
7. Talk over the problem with a trusted confidant.
8. Be optimistic and find ways to solve the problem.

Darrin Donnelly says, "You – and only you – control your thoughts. And how you choose to respond to a negative event will determine your outcome." This certainly applies as you begin to evaluate internal problems that may be the cause of some of your anxiety. You could be causing the problem! If this is a problem caused by you, that puts you in control, and makes it possible for you to find a resolution. It also makes you the one responsible for implementing the actions needed to resolve the problem. Whether the problem is internal or external, you are the one in control and the person responsible for finding solutions.

After having reviewed each of the problems you face, try to determine how to deal with them successfully. Prioritize them in a list from most important to least. Under each problem write your idea for its resolution. Always take one at a time, and don't magnify the problem by compiling several problems into one massive issue. As you develop resolutions for each problem, check that each is directly related to helping manifest your new vision; that is the reason you are doing this difficult exercise in the first place. Once you have identified potential solutions for your problems, focus only on the solutions. The solutions are what will stimulate positive emotions and give you hope for the future. They are what will help you create a pathway to your new vision.

Resolving your problems is crucial in being able to accomplish your dreams and manifest your new vision. The process for change is very simple:

1. Select your dreams.
2. Eliminate the problems.
3. Create your new vision.
4. Set the goals that will help you manifest your vision.

Approach this process with confidence. If you are optimistic about solving the problems, you will solve them. If you solve the problems, you make realizing your dreams much more possible. And when you begin to see your dreams enter into your plans for the future, you will know that your new vision will bring about the changes needed to build your wonderfully exciting new life.

VISUALIZE FREELY

Seeing differently is like putting on an imaginary pair of special glasses and filtering the information through them. Your life is what it is. What is different is what glasses you choose to decide how you want to see the same things differently.

—Ayse Birsel

What does your dream look like? Where does it take place and who is sharing it with you? How does it feel to be in that place with that person? Visualize it. Pretend you are there. Place it in your mind, and soon it will become part of your subconscious. That's where it should be. From there it can influence you until your vision is realized. We need to have a vision to guide the decisions we make. The vision is the destination towards which our road map of life is plotted.

Your vision does not start with analytics. It does not begin by studying the numbers. It starts in your mind and follows the fantasies that motivate you to act. It incorporates your wishes and dreams with an inspired imagination. This is the fun part of planning – the unrestricted, open-ended possibilities to plan without anything in your way. Life will give you all kinds of roadblocks along the way. Life will say no. It will say, "You can't do that." It is up to you to talk back, and say, "Yes, I can."

The stronger your vision is, the more committed you will be to it, and the stronger the possibilities are for realizing that vision. Starting with a blank canvas or an empty piece of paper can be intimidating, especially when it holds the possibilities of a future project or an important plan. But if you have unleashed your imagination, unlocked your dreams and desires and are beginning to form a glimpse of your preferred future, the visualization process will have a head start. When your desires and dreams excite you and become your motivation, a picture of your new life model becomes more in focus.

Developing a vision can take place in all kinds of planning – life planning, project planning, even vacation planning, directing a play, or coaching a sports team. Seeing your vision first allows you to see the strategies you will use, the tactics you need to achieve that vision. Seeing your vision at the onset will provide the enthusiasm to help you move forward through whatever adversity stands in your way. When your vision originates from your dreams and wishes, you have more of a commitment to achieving it. You have created the plan and all of its details, and the planning experience makes the vision more desirable, perhaps almost an obsession. This knowledge and intimate understanding of your vision will enhance your commitment to making it become a reality.

Everyone's life is a blank canvas. It is up to each of us to choose the colors and the image for a perfect picture. Each of us is the artist of our life and can paint the picture that is our vision. There are many ways of making this comparison, but Brian Tracy says it simply: "The person you see is the person you will be."

There is a law in psychology that if you form a picture in your mind of what you would like to be, and you keep and hold that picture there long enough, you will soon become exactly as you have been thinking.

—William James

LIVE WITH INTENTION

You never finish designing your life—life is a joyous and never-ending design project of building your way forward.

—Bill Burnett

Who governs your thinking? Who governs what you see? Who determines what you hear? Who regulates how you feel? Let's hope it's you. If you are the designer of your life, then you have the right and responsibility to make these choices. Look back at your values, your beliefs, and your principles, and see how they can guide your decisions.

All your decisions are influenced by how you want to feel. If you want to feel joy and happiness each day and at every moment, then you must make the decision to live with intention. Living with intention means that your decisions and actions are guided by your values and beliefs. You will be the judge of what you see, hear, and feel. You will be guided by the following statements of belief:

1. When I open my eyes, I intend to be selective about the things that I see. I will choose what I see and select those visions that will bring me joy and happiness every day.
2. When I open my ears to the many voices around me, I will choose to listen to those voices that speak the truth, that speak with compassion for humankind and reinforce my desire to live a joyful and happy life.

3. When I open my mind to the experiences of life, I will select those experiences that reinforce the feelings I wish to have and heighten the joy and happiness of my life.

You have the right and personal responsibility to control your life and to set the stage for optimum joy and happiness. It is your decision. Perhaps your life purpose is to live a life of accomplishment or to dedicate your life to your family, your community, your profession, your country, or your cause. Whatever your purpose, you are in control of encouraging its success. Every action you take will be done with intention, making selections about what to see, hear and feel and what influences your thinking and reinforces your search to accomplish your purpose. To reach success in accomplishing your purpose, let's revisit the following outline:

1. Understand who you are.
2. Define your values, beliefs, and principles.
3. Remember your purpose in life and how you want to feel.
4. See, hear, and be influenced only by what will reinforce your desired feelings and life purpose.
5. Make the commitment to live with intention.

Living a beautiful life can be simple. But it takes time to reflect, to become self-aware and understand who you are and what you want to accomplish. Self-understanding will be a powerful realization and will help you make decisions that support your purpose in life and allow you to succeed in your mission.

Too often, I think, people see the fulfillment of a wish as a consummation, as the end of a process. But doesn't it make more sense to see a wish coming true as a beginning, as the start of something? The real excitement and the real fulfillment lie in seeing where that wish can lead.

—Peter Buffet

LIVE IN TWO WORLDS

Human beings are often, perhaps more often, drawn by the future than they are driven by the past, and so a science that measures and builds expectations, planning, and conscious choice will be more potent than a science of habits, drives, and circumstances. That we are drawn by the future rather than just driven by the past is extremely important and directly contrary to the heritage of social science and the history of psychology. It is, nevertheless, a basic and implicit premise of positive psychology.

—Martin Seligman

We all live in two worlds, the present reality, and the future we imagine. We are constantly torn between these two worlds. One world keeps us at task to accomplish the work of the day, while the other allows our dreams and aspirations to flourish. Moving from one world to the other can be difficult because we are always drawn back to the comfortable, the convenient routines of the past and present. Why change, when the current situation isn't too bad? A little bad, maybe, but not too bad.

It is difficult to cast aside the things we do every day, those routines that keep us going and accomplishing the basic needs of life. However, the basic needs are just that – basic. To have an exciting life, one that is filled with achievements and accomplishments, we need to move to the next phase, the next world, to the vision we create for our future. According to Stephen Covey, "Begin with the end in mind." Covey based this on his conviction that everything is created twice. First, there is the creation phase where we imagine the end results. Second is the physical phase where we bring the image into reality.

To paraphrase Buckminster Fuller again, our objective is to create a vision for the future that is so advanced, so well designed, so exciting, that it makes our current reality obsolete and undesirable. It is much easier to move toward something than it is to move away from something. If we dedicate time to create a vision for the future and make it so wonderful that we have no choice but to adopt it, we have accomplished setting the stage for a perfect transition.

Just like every person, every business exists in two worlds – the world of the present (colored by the past) and the world of the future. I recently attended a presentation by a CEO of a Fortune 500 company in which he talked about change as an imperative. He created a vision for the future of the company as he sees it, explaining with great clarity the problems and opportunities his industry faces. It was wonderful to see how unclouded his vision of the future was and how the company could move forward to accomplish it.

He pointed out that changes in business need to be transitional, because of the requirements of the current reality. Business production requirements, customer needs and buying patterns may or may not change rapidly. His vision, guided by new technologies, may need to be implemented over time, as the company and its customers adapt. With an understanding of the current reality, changing conditions and emerging social patterns, the new vision needs to be constantly modified. These are the two worlds – reality as it exists today and a new vision of the future.

For an individual as well, change may need to be transitional, because a satisfying clean break with the past may not be possible or wise. Certain tasks and routines may still be needed. But as long as we have and sustain a clear vision of our new life and new future, we can bring the driving force within to bear; it will allow us to accomplish every dream, every desire and every hope for a new future.

While building the new future vision, you might actually paint a picture of the new reality you intend to create. If we can imagine it and we can define the details of the new vision, we should be able to paint or draw a picture of ourselves being in that vision – perhaps a room filled with all the things that are part of that vision. Or perhaps a collage with cutouts of all those new things. If we can see it, we can enhance our belief in it, and therefore, it can become a reality and be quite achievable.

IF WE CAN ENVISION IT, WE CAN BELIEVE IT.
IF WE BELIEVE IT, WE CAN ACCOMPLISH IT.

What is your vision for your future? What dreams would you like to integrate into your new future? What are some of the details within your dreams? Can you picture them? How does it feel to be in your dream, your vision? Perhaps painting a picture of your vision will work for you. Perhaps making an outline of your vision will capture all the details and activities that you would like to have in that vision. Maybe mind-mapping would allow you to place all the details of your new vision in a network of connected relationships. Perhaps filling a "vision box" with pictures of people, places, and things, words and stories will help you clarify your vision. However you create your vision, know that it is critical to adopt change and to start moving toward building a new vision that will allow your life to be filled with worthy achievements, exciting adventures and cherished relationships.

We live in two worlds, and it is up to us to design our own lives, our own futures, and our own vision. It is up to us to make the decisions and have the vision for an exciting life filled with achievements and accomplishments and lots of fun along the way.

You turn and you go toward the positive, not away from the negative.

—Emily Fletcher

CHOOSE THE RIGHT WALL

Management is efficiency in climbing the ladder of success, leadership determines whether the ladder is leaning against the right wall.

—Stephen Covey

Imagine it's the end of April and you and your family are making plans for a summer vacation. Discussions begin. Maps are purchased. Tour books are reviewed, and online searches begin. But hold on. What do you want to experience? Are you headed in the right direction? Typically, the choice becomes a matter of negotiations, of a little give and take, but finally a compromise is reached, and a decision is made. Maybe you're going back to the coastal community you have visited time and again because it feels more comfortable than adventuring into new territories. Sound familiar? Sure. We all do it, but unfortunately this approach does not lead to new experiences and fresh adventures.

In our businesses and in our lives, we tend to continue doing what we have always been doing. In our business we fine tune our processes and make improvements, we put things on our priority lists, we track our time, and we research time management techniques. In our personal lives, we tend to go to the same restaurants, meet with the same friends and go to the same entertainment venues, year after year. In your business and in your personal life, have you dedicated time to ask the most basic question? Why? Why am I doing what I am doing? Why have I chosen this business to be in? Sometimes we forget about the most important question. Why are we doing what we are doing?

When we experience a slowdown in business, the first thing that we do is try to increase our customer base and reduce overhead to balance our financials. But the more important approach might be to, first, find out why there is a slowdown. Maybe customers are leaving for a good reason, a reason you can affect. We better find out what that reason is before we are guided by false assumptions and head down the wrong path. In the words of Henry Ford, "If you always do what you've always done, you'll always get what you've always got." Or as Stephen Covey says, the ladder might be leaning against the wrong wall. When we face a slowdown in business, we can work hard, worry too much, blame the sales department, only to find that we are working on the wrong problem. A lot of time and effort can be put into working on the wrong problem. So, from the very start, let's think clearly about what it is that we really want for our business or our personal life. Make sure that our efforts, our research, and our analysis are directed at the correct problem. As we climb the ladder of success, let's make sure that it is leaning against the right wall, the wall that will bring us happiness and the one that will allow us to attain the achievements that are important to us.

A time will come when we need to change directions. We don't need to continue on the same path, especially when that path is going in the wrong direction. In order to select the right path or the right wall, we need to create a clear vision of our preferred future. We need to define the goals that we want to reach in search of that future. And we need to do the appropriate research and discovery to be able to define the process needed for implementation. The most important decision to make is to know where you are going. Always. Without that you are constantly running along the wrong path or climbing the wrong ladder.

What is most exciting about this concept is that as we make choices defined by our dreams and desires and unleashed by our imagination, we can create any future we want. Whether it is a family vacation, a new business opportunity or the desire to meet new friends, we need to start with what we want and why we want it. Then we can start the process of achieving our goals. The more excited we are about our new vision, the more potential there will be for it to succeed. We will make a commitment. We will approach its manifestation with a passion. We will be all in. The ladder is on the right wall, and we are climbing with a fury.

So, before you get totally involved with the process, with management principles, time sheets and tour guides, take time to reach deep into your mind to unleash your true desires. Let these desires influence your major decisions – the process will be much more satisfying, and the results will be targeted to your desired goals and aspirations. Think clearly, unleash your imagination, and embrace change.

Change will not come if we wait for some other person or some other time. We are the ones we've been waiting for. We are the change that we seek.

—Barack Obama

CREATE YOUR VISION

Good business leaders create a vision, articulate the vision, passionately own the vision, and relentlessly drive it to completion.

—Jack Welch

Unless you know what you are looking for, you will never find it. This is such a simple idea, but it is one of the most important reasons that people are not living a life of happiness and excitement. So many people continue to complain that their life is not what they want it to be – their job, their marriage, their social life, their health – yet many have not taken the time to determine what they really want. There is a hole in that kind of thinking. The process designers use to identify problems, understand causes, create a new vision, and take action works much better, and it works for all of us:

1. Determine what the problems are.
2. Find out why they are problems.
3. Figure out what is causing the problems.
4. Unleash your imagination to determine possible options to resolve the problems.
5. Create a vision for your preferred future.
6. Set goals that will help you reach your new future.
7. Develop an action plan to get from your current reality to your preferred future.
8. Achieve your goals and evaluate your new reality.
9. Determine how your new reality can be improved and start the process over again.

Change is constant. We are never finished designing our lives. Once we have determined the problems in our life and have found ways to improve them and succeeded in achieving a new reality, it is time to reevaluate once again from a new position and with new criteria. Our employment, family composition, health, finances, and many other factors continue to change throughout our lives. Consequently, we need to change with them. This can be a frightening realization, but at the same time it can release many anxieties that you may have in beginning the planning process.

Knowing that your plan may only cover a period of a few years, takes off some of the pressure of trying to make it perfect. Perfection is impossible, yet we all try to achieve it. Knowing that our plan can and will change in a reasonable period of time keeps us from being concerned about making a mistake, because the plan can always be changed. In fact, it should be changed, because life changes.

Your beliefs and values help to shape your life and influence decisions that you will make. These beliefs and values are key to forming your life philosophy. These become major guides in your planning process. However, within these philosophical guidelines, you can fill in the blanks with all sorts of details that can change your daily life, form new paths for achieving your goals, and bring new experiences and excitement into your life.

In *Simple Steps to Impossible Dreams,* Steven K. Scott says, "If you don't have a clear picture of your destination and a precise map to get there, you won't even begin the trip." What process can you use to create a new clear vision for your life? Life planning experts have a variety of techniques to get you started. Here are some approaches for creating your vision:

DRAW A PICTURE. Take out a piece of paper and draw a picture of your new vision. Draw anything in the picture – places, people, desired items, location, employment, etc. Once the picture is complete, you will be able to easily see all the things that you feel are important to you in re-designing your life. You will have created a new place, filled with all your desires and dreams.

WRITE YOUR STORY. Become the author of your life. If you enjoy writing, start on a journey to write the story of your vision for life. Fill in all the details. Create an exciting story of the most important person in your life – you. This can be a very exciting adventure, and it will allow you to do a mind drop without hesitation, knowing that these are only words and they can be changed as you edit your life story from time to time.

MAKE YOUR LISTS. Make out lists of all the things that you want as part of your life. In the appendix of this book and at the end of many of the chapters, there are samples of lists that you could work with to guide your planning. Determine the type of lists that are important to your situation and have fun filling them out. They may include a list of your dreams, hopeful achievements, legacies that you want to leave, problems that you are facing, people you want as part of your life and new employment desires. This can be fun and revealing. By unleashing your imagination, all kinds of things can come to the surface. You can list the exciting adventures that you are looking forward to, determine what stands in the way, and plan out ways to get to your new reality.

USE A VISION BOX. Select a box to use and throughout your planning process, place pictures of places you want to go, types of people you wish to interact with, things you want to purchase, homes you would love to live in, and perhaps, a picture of a healthy you. Drop in quotes that have meaning to you, objects that have meaning to you, things that you have written that provide insights and ideas that you have formed throughout your discovery process. As you compile photographs and ideas of your desired future, you will generate concepts of where you want to be and how you could begin planning the paths to get there. Notice what's not in the box. There are things that will need to be left behind, routines to be changed, and obstacles to be dealt with. But, with a view of your new future, you will have a clearer picture of your desired future and be able to approach the planning process with enthusiasm.

WRITE YOUR OWN CURRICULUM. Charles Lutwidge Dodgson, an Oxford scholar better known as Lewis Carroll, the author of *Alice in Wonderland*, suggested that one way to begin self-improvement is to write your own personal curriculum. When you went to college you selected a major course of study and made selections of courses in your curriculum. Consider the possibility of writing the curriculum of your life. What experiences do you wish to have? What do you want to learn?

What ideas do you wish to integrate into your current and future reality? If you look at your life as a college curriculum, what would you include in that experience?

Using one of the planning approaches that I mentioned will help you bring clarity to your desired future. Remember, you are the designer of your life. You are the one that makes the decisions.

Now let's change direction for a moment and think about how we can make our vision a reality. Esther and Jerry Hicks believe that when you have a clear vision of what you want, the "Law of Attraction," will make that vision happen. How is that possible? They believe that because you have clearly defined your goals or desires, your subconscious mind will allow opportunities to manifest. And eventually, because of your actions and decisions, you will receive what it is that you desire. In a sense you will make it happen because of your heightened awareness and your new grasp of opportunities around you.

The real key to this concept is that when your beliefs are so clear and your desire for them so defined in your mind, you will be guided, inspired, and led to that which you seek. You have created the target, you can see the target and, therefore, you will be able to see opportunities which present themselves. The Hickses say,

> Once you understand that you are the creator of your experience, then you will want to identify more clearly what you desire so that you may allow it into your experience…. Nothing comes to you unless you invite it through your thoughts.

Wayne Muller says in *How, Then, Shall We Live?* "Plant what you love in the garden of your life…. What harvest when it comes will bring in great joy?" It's a wonderful concept – thinking about your life within a defined parameter and only putting into your life that which will bring you great joy. In whatever planning process you use, this idea is one that fits. Make the decision about what you will place in your life, your garden. Make the decision about what you don't want in your garden. And when the weeds and obstacles stand in the way of growing your most perfect garden, pull them out, so they do not get in the way of a life full of great joy.

As human beings, our greatness lies not so much in being able to remake the world...but in being able to remake ourselves.

—Gandhi

MEASURE WELL-BEING

I used to think that the topic of positive psychology was happiness, that the gold standard for measuring happiness was life satisfaction, and the goal of positive psychology was to increase life satisfaction. I now think that the topic of positive psychology is well-being, that the gold standard for measuring well-being is flourishing, and that the goal of positive psychology is to increase flourishing.

—Martin Seligman

What is your purpose in life? What is it that brings your life value, satisfaction or meaning? Seligman believes that five elements influence a state of well-being: positive emotion, engagement, meaning, positive relationships, and accomplishment. These are his five "pillars." In *Flourishing,* Seligman says that to attain well-being, we need to understand how each of these pillars is defined in our personal life and how each influences our decisions. Recognizing the importance of these and using them as a guide for planning will magnify the chances for a life of satisfaction and fulfillment, enhance our state of happiness and reinforce our life contentment. We need to look deeply into each of these and find how each influences our current life and future vision. Realizing that each of these elements have a part to play in our life planning and in our actions, we need to define the impact that each will have on our life.

POSITIVE EMOTION. Approaching life with optimism and a positive spirit is one of the most important elements. We must believe in our future. We must feel that what we are planning for our life will have positive outcomes. This will allow us to proceed with confidence and to unleash our dreams and desires without reservation. Being positive and optimistic will automatically set the stage for happy results. Will a positive spirit guarantee good results? Of course not. But, if we approach life with an optimistic and positive spirit, one thing is assured – we will enjoy the process along the way, whether we reach our goals or not. Happiness is not the end goal. It is the way, as so many philosophers have said. An optimistic spirit allows us to have confidence that we can realize our dreams. When we are in this spirit, planning becomes a platform for a joyful experience.

ENGAGEMENT AND MEANING. But a positive emotion does not stand alone. As Victor Frankl says in *Man's Search for Meaning,* life involves much more than merely a happy existence. We, as human beings, need to feel that our life has a purpose and that our beliefs and actions connect with a greater meaning. Additionally, we need to understand the reasons why we believe and do things. Life is more than our current, day-to-day reality. Life needs to have significance, and therefore our actions must have meanings. Connecting with a cause provides us with a purpose, and that begins to introduce meaning into our lives. Once we know our life purpose and the meaning it has, we can become engaged in pursuing activities that help support our purpose. Engagement gets us connected and involved with the outcomes and can impact the positive purpose of our cause.

POSITIVE RELATIONSHIPS. Involving ourselves with people who have similar beliefs and life objectives will help reinforce our actions. Have you surrounded yourself with people who support your beliefs? If not, why not? Life is too short to maintain the agonies of negative relationships. Selecting your team of friends and associates is a vital decision that you must make. I use the word "team" purposefully, because if you surround yourself with positive thinking people, they become a support team for you and reinforce the decisions that control your actions. Negative forces are a drain on your system and will keep you from making the decisions to expedite your purpose in life. Choose your relationships carefully and with purpose. Who will support your ideas and dreams? Who will help launch and continue to support your purpose in life?

ACCOMPLISHMENT. The result of all the planning, introspection, relationship development and personal understanding is the success you will have in your personal accomplishments. Successful accomplishments validate your life's purpose and the actions and goals you have defined. Knowing your purpose, understanding why you are here on this earth, and defining how your actions can leave a legacy culminates in your accomplishments. Finally, here is a summary of the progression of thinking inspired by Seligman, Frankl, and many others:

Approach life with positive emotions that support your life's purpose and meaning. Become engaged with purposeful activities and surround yourself with supportive relationships that help you achieve your goals. In two sentences, this summarizes and connects the most important approaches to a balanced and satisfying life. Always stay positive. Always stay optimistic. You will attract into your life what you are thinking about and dreaming about. Positive thoughts attract positive results.

UNLEASH YOUR NEW VISION: TWELVE STEPS

From previous lists and worksheets, select your most important decisions and discoveries to answer many of the questions in these twelve steps to create and refine your new vision.

1. List your most important dreams and desires.
2. Determine how you would like to feel.
3. List your most important interests, talents and skills.
4. List your most important values and beliefs.
5. List what makes you enthused and excited.
6. List activities and experiences you wish to do or have.
7. Identify who you would like to be with.
8. List new achievements you want to accomplish.
9. Envision your future in each important area of your life.
10. List your new desires and intentions for each area of your life.
11. Resolve or modify the problems that stand in your way.
12. Create a vision for your new life.

UNLEASH YOUR NEW VISION WORKSHEET

You are working to take charge of your life and make decisions that will help you reach your preferred future. These questions will help you sort and select the goals and aspirations that form a vision for your new life.

What would you like to have in your new life – your most important dreams and desires?

1._____

2._____

3._____

4._____

5._____

How would you like to feel on a daily basis in your new life?

1._____

2._____

3._____

4._____

5._____

What makes you enthused and excited? What activities would you like to include in your new life?

1._____

2._____

3._____

4._____

5._____

What would you like to change or eliminate in your new life?

1._____

2._____

3._____

4._____

5._____

What would you like to achieve, professionally, in your new life? What are the three most important?

1._____

2._____

3._____

Who you would like to be with, and who would support your new vision?

1._____

2._____

3._____

4._____

5._____

What will you include in your new vision for each area of your life (family, personal, professional, financial, health, cultural and spiritual)?

1._____

2._____

3._____

4._____

5._____

Select the most important actions in your new vision and write them as an advantage statement. Example: I plan to purchase a new, larger home for my growing family in a location with better educational opportunities for my children.

1. _____

   _____

   _____

2. _____

   _____

   _____

3. _____

   _____

   _____

eight

LIVE YOUR VISION

BUILD AN EXCEPTIONAL LIFE

Your destination is determined by what you focus on. You have to be very clear about where you want to go. Once you know where you want to go, you have to visualize yourself getting there and forget about all the places where you don't want to end up.

—Darrin Donnelly

WE HAVE TALKED ABOUT USING IMAGINATION and creativity to design an exciting life, but another process I suggest is using step-by-step thinking to help formulate a powerful life vision. Here are the steps for achieving that.

UNLEASH YOUR IMAGINATION

The first step toward building an exciting life is to open your mind and free your imagination.

- Whose life do you want to lead?
- What influences are shaping your life at this time?
- Is this the life that you feel comfortable with? If not, then you need to take the first step in defining your future, because it is your future.

This is the time to think freely about all those things you want in your life, the places that you want to visit and the people you want to associate with on a daily basis. It is the time to dream about the possibilities – working in a resort on the shores of California or the French Riviera, completing an advanced degree from a prestigious university, spending a year as a plein air painter in Barcelona, creating a charitable institution in support of autistic children or building an online business that uses your experience and training. There are all kinds of possibilities. You are only limited by the depth of your imagination. This is your life. Create it.

HARNESS YOUR DREAMS

Dreaming is exciting. But harnessing your dreams brings them into reality. We spend enormous amounts of time planning, making out our lists and getting ready for the future. The future is now, in this present moment. In this sense, there is no tomorrow. Implement the steps needed to bring those dreams into reality and start living them now. A plan is just a plan, a dream is just a dream, but when you create the action steps for implementing those dreams, you begin to live your dreams and enrich your life. It is your life. You have created the dreams. You have used your imagination to unleash your inner desires. Now it is time to use your planning skills, use your lists of wants and desires, and plot a course to bring your dreams into reality. This is the most exciting part of the planning process. It is the most unencumbered. And it brings an authenticity to the next steps of planning your most exciting life.

DISCOVER YOUR WHY

During your first steps in this process, you have uncovered things you may not have thought about for some time. You may have brought hidden desires to the surface. And in this process, you have thought a lot about who you are, who you want to be, who you want to be with and where you would like to live or work. In the process of making your wish lists, you need to ask one question for each wish – why? Why do you want to live in California? Why do you want to finish an advanced degree? Why do you want to create an institution supporting autistic children? Answering these questions will help shape your value system.

What are the values that motivate you to want the things on your dream list? Are your values centered around charity, peace, spirituality, aesthetics, compassion, excellence, ambition? To take the next step toward defining your exciting life, you need to ask the "why" question about every one of your desires and then begin to list the values in your life that have influenced those dreams. This will give you a good basis for the next step, which is defining your beliefs.

This entire process is a method of understanding yourself.

- Who are you?
- What drives you toward your desires?
- What are you living for?

Answering the "why" to almost any question will lead you to accurate answers and provide you with reasons for your choices.

DEFINE YOUR BELIEFS

We go through life, day by day, following the same routine and making decisions for ourselves and our family and performing to the best of our ability at work. We make decisions based on our preferences, prejudices, and beliefs. In an earlier chapter, I asked you to make a list of all your beliefs. Writing down your beliefs is vital to understanding who you are. Our beliefs can be abstract ideas or true convictions, and as we make decisions throughout the day, those decisions are influenced by these beliefs. If we clearly identify these beliefs and see their relationship to one another, we could begin to understand why we make certain decisions and choices, but most of all, we could understand who we really are and what we stand for.

Reviewing these beliefs gives us a much better idea of who we are as a husband or wife, as parents or grandparents, as business owners, as professionals and as citizens in our community. It helps us clarify why we do things and why we make the decisions we do. It is a wonderful way to transition into the next steps of clarifying our purpose and refining our philosophy.

CLARIFY YOUR PURPOSE

Through this process you have opened your mind by using your imagination and revealing your most important dreams and desires. And you have begun to think about how many of these you could bring into reality. You have probably set some goals or at least a list of some that you would like to accomplish. You have dug deep into your subconscious to reveal your core values, the things that are important to you, your family, your business and how you relate to others. From these values you have been able to establish your beliefs, the most critical part of your self-evaluation. Now it's time to make some connections.

- Why are your beliefs important?
- What can you do to make those beliefs have an impact and guide you to a more meaningful life?

Finding your purpose in life is the result of your evaluation. Your values always play a part in the ways you choose to use your expertise and ambition to make a difference for your community, your country, and your world. Review your list of beliefs.

- Which of those beliefs rises to the surface to become a core value?
- How can these help you define your purpose?

Your purpose is the culmination of all of your thinking and your self-evaluation. Your purpose, then, enables you to begin to develop your roadmap for accomplishing your purposeful goals. With all of the reinforcement gained by defining your beliefs and values, you have the ammunition to begin feeling the passion – the passion to accomplish your life's purpose.

REFINE YOUR PHILOSOPHY

We have heard of the elevator speeches that many businesses use to describe their business philosophy, products, or services. Often, these are derived from the company leadership and are meant to describe, in a sentence or two, the company's reasons for being in business, commitment to their customers and to the quality of products or services rendered. Can you use this thinking to write a personal elevator speech? We are the CEOs of our own lives, so it is up to us to create that elevator speech. Perhaps, instead of an elevator speech, we can consider it our creed, the core of our life philosophy.

Your life philosophy is a culmination of your dreams, your beliefs and your life purpose and integrates the answers to your personal "why" that we discussed earlier.

- What is your driving motivation that supports your mission?
- What wakes you up in the morning excited about the challenges awaiting you?
- What actions are well integrated with your values and beliefs?
- What are you passionate about?

All these feelings can be embodied in your personal philosophy. Once you articulate your philosophy, it can be the guiding light that helps you make the critical decisions in your daily life as well as your long-term goals and aspirations. You have a philosophy. It already drives your decisions in life. It is what you think about before you communicate with others. It governs why you do things. If we can clarify our statement of philosophy, we will have a much better understanding of what motivates us. All you need to do is set a little time aside to reflect, think, imagine, and unlock the wonderful qualities within you.

WRITE YOUR CREED

You have already listed your principles in your core values, in your beliefs, in your life's purpose and in your personal philosophy. Is it possible to bring all this thinking together to make a statement of ultimate belief in a personal life creed? This may take a little time and analysis, but the connections need to be made in order to develop a statement of your personal creed. Every religion, fraternity, and service club has a creed that governs the beliefs and actions of their followers. You may recall your religious creed. This may be a good model to follow for developing your personal creed. How can you connect your most important values and integrate them into a statement?

Your creed is the summary of who you are, what you believe and your life's purpose. Create it and be guided by it throughout your life.

BUILD YOUR VISION

All these discoveries are extremely helpful in developing a new vision for your life. As you finalize your thinking, be sure that each of the elements in this process reinforce your new vision. If your values and beliefs are congruent with your actions, your life will be in harmony. You have spent much time self-evaluating and discovering things from your past that have helped to form your current beliefs. Use these as you build your future. If you work with this honest and authentic approach, your results will have a better chance of succeeding and providing you with a spectacular life.

EMBRACE PRAXIS AND CONGRUENCY

'Praxis' ... means the integration of your beliefs with your behavior.

—John Assaraf

Simply stated, praxis is putting your ideas and theories into practice. According to Merriam-Webster, praxis is the "practical application of a theory." Praxis reminds us of the transformative nature of action, and as the Oxford English Dictionary says, is "the synthesis of theory and practice, without presuming the primacy of either." For those of us wishing to give our lives greater unity, power and direction, praxis is essential. So is its parallel concept, congruency. Carl Rogers refers to congruency as a state in which a person's ideal self and actual experience are consistent or analogous. In geometry, congruency means two shapes or objects with the same shape and size; they may be mirror images of each other. To apply this to what we are studying, try unleashing your imagination and unlocking those desires buried in your subconscious or buried in your past. Realize that the process of self-understanding and creating a vision of your future is not simple. It is divided into several parts, all of which need to be gone through to have a successful outcome.

GRASP REALITY

First, come to grips with your current reality. This means clearly understanding your existing situation and the problems that get in the way of your aspirations. It means looking closely at your responsibilities, the people you interact with every day, and the challenges of your normal routines. Fully understanding the conditions in which you live is vital to seeing what obstacles inhibit your personal growth.

DISCARD OBSTACLES

Next, identify each of the obstacles causing a problem and work to ignore, modify or remove them from your life. This involves an honest appraisal of responsibilities, work requirements, personal relationships, financial positions, and many other factors that could play a part in holding you back from making progress. Make out a list of these obstacles. Categorizing them as family, professional, financial, spiritual, personal, health or cultural, etc., may help you understand them and decide what action to take.

ARRIVE AT ZERO

To proceed to the creative thinking process, we must reach a point where all our obstacles are realized and understood. They are identified and written down on paper to see and review. We need to see which are the most troublesome, which have the most potential for change, and which can be dispensed with immediately. We need to get to a point of clarity, to arrive at a zero point, where, while we may not have moved forward yet, no obstacles stand in our way. Experiencing this kind of clarity and freedom will let us open our mind and unleash our imagination in search of a new future.

UNLEASH YOUR IMAGINATION

The dreams, the desires and the hopes are now ready to be unleashed. Our mind is free, obstacles have been managed, and our mind is clear, uncluttered, and ready to imagine the possibilities. In the process of unleashing our imagination, we are free to harness our beliefs, values, and principles and let these influence our plans for the future. When we free ourselves from the clutter of responsibilities, duties chosen for us by others, and routines, we open ourselves to a world of possibilities.

CREATE YOUR VISION

After taking the previous steps, it is much simpler to make plans for our future. Using all our lists of dreams and desires and knowing what we want our future to be, we can begin reinventing ourselves and our future to be in accordance with the true desires we have identified.

TAKE ACTION

The final step in this process is to bring our vision into reality. Mapping out how we want to implement our vision, plan a schedule of our own, change our life and set goals for accomplishing our vision will be part of making our vision a reality.

Throughout this process we are planning our life in an authentic manner, starting from our current reality, cleaning the slate, unleashing our dreams, building our perfect future, and taking action to accomplish our vision. This can be a simple process, but it is filled with details and decisions to make. Here is where the concepts of praxis and congruency are relevant. A future vision developed through an honest self-discovery process and one that truly opens our imagination to discover our dreams and desires will provide us with a more accurate appraisal of who we are and where we want to be. Planning a life based on our values and beliefs and incorporating our dreams and desires places us in a perfect position to reach a life of congruency, where beliefs and actions are parallel. When we reach this place, our life is in a more perfect harmony.

If we were composers of music, harmony would be achieved when all the notes had a balanced relationship and the notes, when combined into a chord, create a pleasant, soothing sound. When the notes are not in harmony, but are dissonant, the results can be disturbing and difficult to hear. The same is true for one's life. If we have both a life purpose and an action plan to achieve that purpose, we are working in harmony and the result is a more natural flow of ideas and actions – praxis, an agreement of philosophy and practice.

A key ingredient to achieving your goals is to make sure your goals are totally congruent with who you are as a person. Your head and your heart's desire must match. It's such an important step in goal achievement, and if we miss it, we can end up traveling a long way down the wrong path.

—Rachael Birmingham

PURSUE HAPPINESS

Whether this moment is happy or not depends on you. It's you who makes the moment happy, not the moment that makes you happy. With mindfulness, concentration, and insight, any moment can become a happy moment.

—Thich Nhat Hanh

Happiness is not a place in the future. It is not a goal. It is a way of life. When your beliefs, goals and actions are in alignment, you will be living in true happiness. Happiness is different for everyone because we all have different beliefs. Our beliefs drive our ambitions. Our beliefs influence our goals and allow us to define our objectives. Our beliefs are the source of our purpose in life.

For you, happiness may be working on an ambitious professional goal. It may be sitting in solitude by a gently flowing stream. It may be attending a baseball game with your son or daughter or enjoying a musical performance. All happiness happens now, because now is the only time we have. Yesterday can be a fond memory. Tomorrow is a dream filled with desire and possibilities. But happiness is experienced today, at this moment. "Happiness is not a goal, it is the way." It is how we design our way of life. It is the spirit in which we interact with others. It is the love of being alive and being able to experience the excitement of the moment. Happiness can be enjoyed every moment of our life. An artist friend of mine once said that we find happiness through the joyful experience of working toward our creative goals.

Thomas Jefferson concluded the Declaration of Independence with the phrase, "life, liberty and the pursuit of happiness." With this document, the pursuit of happiness became a right of the citizens of the United States, but notice that while we have the right to pursue happiness, it is up to us to achieve it. This requires understanding what makes us happy.

When your values, beliefs and actions are congruent, you are in a state of praxis, and this brings true happiness to your life. There is no conflict in your thinking and your activities, but instead, a consistent and concentric flow. All is right with your life. In one sense, Jefferson didn't go far enough. We don't pursue happiness. We pursue activities, goals and visions that bring about happiness and joy. Most important, the act of pursuing our goals and visions is a joyous and happy experience. In whatever way we define happiness, we need to know that it is not our goal in life to find happiness. It is our goal to experience happiness, excitement, and joy along the way. We need to pursue our goals, respect the preciousness of life, and feel the thrill of being alive.

What makes us happy? Sometimes it is acquiring things we have been wanting for a while, like a new car, a well-planned vacation, or a new piece of furniture. Or it can be the simple joys of hearth and home, a loving relationship with another person or working toward a major goal. Barbara Sher says, "When we understand that the secret to happiness lies not in possessing but in giving, by making others happy, we shall be happier ourselves." Remember, happiness and joy are not things or places but the feelings you get when you live your life's purpose. Finding pleasure in the process is the key. Emily Fletcher says, in *Stress Less, Accomplish More*,

> Who cares if there is a pot of gold at the end of the imaginary rainbow if you're unhappy chasing after it your entire life? Who cares if the destination is amazing if the journey there was terrible? Life is short – why embrace unnecessary misery?

Understanding who you are and identifying your unique values and beliefs are essential to clarifying your approach to life and to finding your state of true happiness and joy. As you have read throughout this book, you have reviewed many aspects of your personal characteristics. You have used your imagination to manifest your most important dreams and desires, and you have understood what influences your life. With this self-knowledge and with a well-defined path toward executing your life's purpose, you can be well on your way to living in a state of well-being.

Yesterday is but a dream and tomorrow is only a vision, but today well lived makes every yesterday a dream of happiness and every tomorrow a vision of hope.

—Khalil Gibran

BE COMPASSIONATE

Those who are without compassion cannot see what is seen with the eyes of compassion.

—Thich Nhat Hanh

We have talked about how we see, how we perceive and how, when our mind is wide open, we are able to unleash our imagination and dream the dreams of hope. Thich Nhat Hanh gives us a strong example of one way to see – through the eyes of compassion. Earlier, I talked about changing the lenses in our glasses and by so doing, adjusting the way we see. If we see our own failure whenever someone else succeeds, our lenses are green with envy. If we are too afraid of failure or ridicule to take action, our lenses are yellow with cowardice. If indecision plagues us, our lenses are fogged over, and we cannot see a clear pathway ahead. If, on the other hand, our lenses are rose-colored, we will perceive everything in our life as beautiful or having the potential for beauty. To our rose-colored glasses, we should add, as Thich Nhat Hanh suggests, seeing with the eyes of compassion.

Seeing with compassion changes our perceptions of people, events, and life itself. Our perceptions are influenced by a loving compassion, and we see the goodness in everything that comes before us. We have a concern for the welfare of all people, and we are sympathetic to those in need. It is a peaceful experience, to shed the shadows of fear, envy or selfishness and see the potential in everyone. With compassion, we seek to help people reach their potential. We see that things are possible, not impossible. We approach every problem with hope and with the assurance that there can be an appropriate solution. And we see the goodness in every person we meet, without prejudice.

Seeing through the eyes of compassion can help us find our dreams and unleash our imagination. There is only one best way to approach life – optimistically. Being positive in every experience, in every decision will, at the very least, bring you peace of mind knowing that you have seen the positive potential in your decisions and you have made every decision knowing that you have given yourself the best chance for successful results. You have seen the future with a positive vision. You will experience the feelings of achievement through your thoughtful decisions, and you can feel confident in your choices and in yourself. Seeing through the eyes of compassion will extend your positive approach by allowing you to see people with the happiness derived from caring.

As you plan your life with all the knowledge that you have gained, I challenge you to bring compassion into your way of thinking and seeing. It will be more compatible with your inner voice – the one that you knew when you were young. It will bring a congruency to your thoughts and actions, and it will reinforce your values, knowing that you have made decisions based on your concern for others and your willingness to harness your principles as a guide. It will allow you to find peace within yourself, in your relationships, and in your actions.

Knowing yourself, knowing who you are and what you believe is essential to finding peace in your life and in your actions. Including compassion in your vision will allow you to see with a vision of hope. Adopting compassion as a core value brings respect for your fellow human beings, whether they are like you or not. All human beings should be able to live freely without fear or conflict. We all can live in peace and friendship. We all need to know that we love and we are loved. Compassion brings confidence, happiness, and joy to our life. It introduces a paradigm reinforcing all that is good. As you bring about change in your life and plan for your future, let a compassionate spirit influence your vision, and let it be a guide to making decisions in your plan.

We are each made for goodness, love and compassion. Our lives are transformed as much as the world is when we live with these truths.... God's dream is that you and I and all of us will realize that we are family, that we are made for togetherness, for goodness and for compassion.

—Desmond Tutu

LIVE IN CONGRUENCY

In short, you stay young in soul by not becoming a fossil in your life. You keep abreast of the world as it advances. You stay fresh in your understanding and values. You say yes to life's invitations.

—Thomas Moore

Living in harmony occurs when your vision and actions are all in alignment. You have reached congruency in all aspects of your life when your purpose is being fulfilled. You have a clear sight of your future, and your vision is being realized every day. Happiness and joy are part of each day of your life, and your ambitions and actions are in alignment.

This harmonious state is different for everyone because we all have had different life experiences. We will, therefore, have different dreams and desires. What is important to one person may not matter to another. So, we need to understand for ourselves what it is that makes us excited about life and to identify our favorite activities. We need to harness our passion and participate in activities that support our purpose. Harmony comes when conflict is eliminated, when problems are solved and when we see a clear path to realizing our vision. When our beliefs are supported by our actions, we are at peace with our purpose, and our life plan is coming together and being realized.

Let's look at three different people and imagine how each one might create a harmonious lifestyle.

JEFFREY IS A FINANCIAL PLANNER. He has always enjoyed mathematics and was a math major in college. He joined a financial planning firm after graduation and absolutely fell in love with the work, finding it rewarding to help clients reach their investment and financial goals. He enjoys problem-solving and has always found pleasure in working analytically. His personal life involves service to the local Rotary club and other organizations. His passion is financial literacy, and he participates in such programs in nearby high schools and colleges. His actions in life are in alignment with his values and purpose, and he feels that he is living in harmony.

KATHERINE IS A PSYCHOLOGIST. She has always loved working with people. Her personality exudes happiness and joy, and her interactions with people are always friendly and supportive. After graduating from a prestigious university with a master's degree in psychology, she joined a nonprofit, where she used her skills and education to help people with addiction. She was so effective that within a short time, she was chosen as the CEO and now provides leadership to a staff of several hundred counselors. Her aspirations are to generate more public support for mental health and eventually to seek a leadership role in government so she can impact national-level problems. Her desire to help people in need, and her leadership abilities are in alignment, and this congruency of purpose and action gives her life harmony.

NATHAN IS AN ARCHITECT. He has enjoyed designing and creating things since he was in grade school and always enjoyed working with virtual building games. In college, he was fascinated with problem-solving and designing beautiful buildings. Upon graduation with a degree in architecture, he began working for an architectural firm in Chicago with an office that had wonderful views of Lake Michigan and the Chicago skyline. He was in designer's heaven—working on projects that enhanced people's lives and using his talents and passion to fulfill his aesthetic objectives. His long-term goal is to found his own architectural firm that specializes in historically accurate restoration. He is on his way to leading the life that he designed. His passion for beauty and his daily activities are in alignment, and his life is in harmony.

All these lives are different, but they all have a common denominator – an alignment of purpose and action. In each case passion for a particular cause is satisfied through daily responsibilities. This congruency allows each of these lives to be in harmony. However, not being in alignment is a sure way of bringing unhappiness to one's life. As Barbara

Sher says, "Nothing creates more stress than when our actions and behavior aren't congruent with our values." When belief and action are not aligned, your daily life is dissonant, and everything may seem pointless. To be happy and find harmony, we need to know exactly what we want and how we are moving toward getting there.

CREATE A LEGACY

The key to real leadership is inspiring others to be leaders. The key to good parenting, and strong relationships, is helping to bring out the best in the people we love. The key to happiness is finding joy in helping others become happier. And the key to achieving your highest potential starts by helping others achieve theirs.

—Shawn Achor

Each of us has a purpose in life; understanding yours is what we have been discussing. Our purpose guides and validates our actions. It brings meaning and importance to our achievements. Your purpose is stronger if it has greater significance. It is stronger if it affects others both now and well into the future. Many great people have committed to a cause throughout their life and have dedicated their life to fulfilling that cause. Consider these inspiring examples:

JONAS SALK committed a period of his life to finding a vaccine for polio, and with this research he saved the lives of millions who, without the vaccine, would have died.

FRANK LLOYD WRIGHT committed his life to architectural design authenticity through organic architecture, and to this day Wright is considered the greatest architect in the United States and perhaps the world. His architectural design theory has permeated architecture and has been a cornerstone of architectural education.

FRANKLIN D. ROOSEVELT rose despite enormous physical obstacles to lead the country and the world through the Great Depression and World

War II. His contributions, leadership and honesty are remembered to this day.

PABLO PICASSO dedicated his life to art and has, through his paintings and sculpture, significantly changed the landscape of art for the twentieth and twenty-first centuries.

RUTH BADER GINSBURG, appointed to the U. S. Supreme Court in 1993, dedicated her life, as a professor, attorney, and judge, to gender equality and the rights of workers. As a young attorney, she argued landmark cases before the Supreme Court that opened the door for the rights of women in the United States.

THOMAS MOORE investigated the impact of our souls on our lives, our beliefs, and our actions. He has written over twenty books, all highly respected and read by millions of followers. He has changed the way people think and allowed his readers to have a better understanding of themselves.

Each one of these leaders has been an inspiration to the world with their dedication to a cause and to mankind. Each left a great legacy and contributed to the betterment of our society. Can you use them or an example of your own choice as inspiration as you seek to define your purpose and your mission? Ask yourself, how will your efforts be remembered after you are gone, and how will those efforts impact our future societies?

These questions can help you determine how to become significant in your lifetime and have your contributions live on to improve the human condition for centuries to come. Answering them can help you put your talents, skills, and beliefs to use to impact future generations. You have already worked to understand yourself better, unleash your imagination, and direct your abilities and talents. Now, look further into the future.

- How will you and your ideas be remembered?

- How can you have a significant impact on others?
- How can you leave a legacy that influences those who come after you?

Answering these questions will take an enormous stretch of imagination and enormous confidence in your abilities.

You are an important person. You have been given a life. You are fortunate enough to have a mind that can think, imagine, and create. These qualities are not to be wasted on insignificant activities. We have gone through exercises where we advance from ordinary to-do lists to lists of achievements, personal feelings, and ways to contribute to society. It is important to select from those lists to see how you can capture that which will be remembered as your dedication to a cause. This could give you more drive and let you live a life with greater purpose. It could change your thinking and your life dramatically. What cause or goal do you feel strongly about, strongly enough to dedicate your life to?

Defining your legacy and deciding how to implement it affects your life in two ways. First, you find that your current life is enriched by working toward your legacy goals. Such goals can help you see beyond yourself. It can make the trials of today seem trivial. Second, you can find peace in knowing that you are making a contribution that will live on into the future. You will be rewarded with the knowledge that you have dedicated your life to helping others in significant ways. In *The Big Shift*, Marc Freeman writes about it this way: "This extended trajectory brings with it a reminder that we need to be thinking longer term, perhaps asking the question that Jonas Salk raised, namely, 'Are we being good ancestors?'"

We all want to feel that our life has relevance and that we can leave this earth knowing that we did as much as we could to advance our civilization. Freeman continues,

The narrative beauty of generativity is that it provides a way of thinking about the end of one's life that suggests that the end is not really the end. I may die, but my children will live on. My own story may end, but other stories will follow mine, due in part to my own generative efforts.

With a legacy defined, we reap the rich rewards of knowing we have done well and have become an important part of the future.

In *The Infinite Game*, Simon Sinek talks about changing our mindset and allowing ourselves to think about our life, not just in the present, but after we leave this earth and as we continue to live through our personal legacy.

> As for us, those who choose to embrace an infinite mindset, our journey is one that will lead us to feel inspired every morning, safe when we are at work and fulfilled at the end of each day. And when it is our time to leave the game, we will look back at our lives and our careers and say, "I lived a life worth living."

Sinek also points out that what he calls "an infinite mindset" lets us foresee a future in which others are inspired to carry on our legacy. These questions may help you focus on how to think about your legacy. Ask yourself,

- How can I make an impact on future generations?
- What can I do to help, support, or inspire future generations?

This simple Greek proverb captures the essence of leaving a legacy: "A society grows great when old men plant trees in whose shade they will never sit."

A COMMON BOND

Each of us is a composite of experiences and influences. Each of us is unique, because no one else on this earth has had the same collection of experiences. At the same time, each of us is connected. Because so many of our experiences are derived from someone else, many others are part of us. We live on the same ground. We breathe the same air. We see the same trees, mountains, and flowers. Because each of us sees with different eyes and experience with different minds, we are unique in spite of our many points of connectivity. Through music, stories, art, and philosophy, we can see through the eyes of others and learn what they believe. By putting aside ego, arrogance, and prejudice, we can grasp truths that bring us together in a common bond of humanity.

We are brothers and sisters in the life experience, and knowing this helps us be at peace with our world and ourselves. Inner peace comes from the realization that we know ourselves and that we are at peace with our philosophy. When our beliefs, our actions, and our goals are all in alignment, we can achieve peace.

Study religion. Study philosophy. Study psychology. Read, read, and read more. Define your beliefs. Determine your why. Find your personal meaning and purpose. These will bring you closer to peace and understanding.

LIFE WITHOUT BOUNDARIES

When I am in an airplane and look down on this beautiful Earth, I do not see lines marking the various states or countries. In its natural setting, our world flows seamlessly from one region to the next. In a similar way, our lives in their natural state do not have boundaries. The more we impose them upon ourselves, the more confusion and self-doubt can weaken us. The more we unleash our imaginations, recognize our own potential, and embark on a thoughtful pursuit of becoming our own best selves, the more we will feel the optimism, peace, and joy of that journey.

Inner peace, mutual understanding, and respect for ourselves and for each other is what each of us wants. These will let us pursue happiness, experience joy, and live in a state of well-being – today and tomorrow.

LIVE YOUR VISION: TWELVE STEPS

In each of the seven areas of your life, make a plan and set goals that incorporate your dreams, desires, feelings, values, beliefs and intended accomplishments.

1. Develop a plan with goals for your personal life.
2. Develop a plan with goals for your family life.
3. Develop a plan with goals for your health.
4. Develop a plan with goals for your finances.
5. Develop a plan with goals for your professional interests.
6. Develop a plan with goals for your spiritual life.
7. Develop a plan with goals for your educational and cultural interests.
8. Prioritize your goals for each area of life.
9. Determine how your decisions will bring happiness and joy to your life.
10. Implement your action plan for each of the seven areas of your life.
11. Decide how you will leave your legacy.
12. Live and enjoy your life in harmony.

LIVE YOUR VISION WORKSHEET

To understand how planning can bring about change, imagine how your life might change if you could live your vision every day and in every way. The following questions will help you fill out the details about how your life will change and how you will feel when you achieve your new vision.

What important changes do you want or need to make in each of these areas of life?

1. Family _____

_____

_____

2. Personal _____

_____

_____

3. Professional _____

_____

_____

4. Financial _____

_____

_____

5. Health _____

_____

_____

6. Cultural _____

_____

_____

7. Spiritual _____

_____

_____

Which of these changes will bring you the most joy and happiness?

1._____

2._____

3._____

How will your relationships change in your new life?

1._____

2._____

3._____

What goals and achievements do you desire most in each area?

1. Family _____

_____

_____

2. Personal _____

_____

_____

3. Professional _____

_____

_____

4. Financial _____

_____

_____

5. Health _____

_____

_____

6. Cultural _____

_____

_____

7. Spiritual _____

_____

_____

Which changes are the most important? Put them in priority order.

1._____

2._____

3._____

4._____

5._____

What actions need to be taken to implement these important changes?

1._____

2._____

3._____

4._____

5._____

What will be your most important achievements and how will they help prepare your legacy?

1._____

2._____

3._____

4._____

5._____

From the lists above, select the three most important achievements you want in your new life, why they are important and how they will affect your future. Write them in a sentence answering each part of the question. Example: I will dedicate time and energy to getting an MBA to gain the knowledge and credentials to advance in my career.

1. _____

_____

_____

2. _____

_____

_____

3. _____

_____

_____

appendix a

LIFE-PLANNING SUMMARY WORKSHEET

At the end of each chapter, you have been asked to answer a series of questions. Bring your answers from each of the previous chapter worksheets to this life-planning summary to create a composite of your thinking. Your answers will provide the basis for planning your new life and defining its details. They will help you take action to implement your vision, refine your life's purpose and achieve your goals.

What are your three most important dreams and desires?

1._____

2._____

3._____

What three feelings do you want most in your life?

1._____

2._____

3._____

What are your three most important values?

1._____

2._____

3._____

What are your three most important beliefs?

1._____

2._____

3._____

What are your three most important principles?

1._____

2._____

3._____

What three things bring meaning to your life?

1._____

2._____

3._____

Write a statement that reflects your philosophy of life.

_____

_____

_____

Write a statement of your purpose in life.

_____

_____

_____

Write a statement of your mission in life.

_____

_____

_____

Write your personal creed.

_____

_____

_____

What are the three most important problems or obstacles you need to act upon?

1._____

2._____

3._____

Define the legacy you would like to leave for future generations.

_____

_____

_____

List what you would like to include in your new life vision.

1. _____

2. _____

3. _____

4. _____

5. _____

6. _____

7. _____

8. _____

9. _____

10. _____

11. _____

12. _____

13. _____

14. _____

15. _____

16. _____

17. _____

18. _____

19. _____

20. _____

The last steps in creating your new life are to develop a chart and timetable for implementing the actions needed for reaching your goals in each important area of your life. Prioritize your goals and actions, connect them with completion dates on your timetable and organize them into a chart for easy reference. It is now time to begin creating your extraordinary, preferred future.

appendix b

EXPANDED SELF-DISCOVERY LISTS

The following is a series of list ideas that include and add to the list suggestions at the end of each chapter. You may want to refer to these additional suggestions as you complete each chapter or use them now to dig deeper or enrich your earlier answers.

ONE/TWO: UNLEASH YOUR DREAMS/FANTASIES

1. List all of your hopes and dreams.
2. List your most important desires.
3. List the things you are curious about.
4. What are new things you want to experience?
5. What do you wish your future could include?
6. What are the things you want to learn?
7. What do you intend to do to manifest your dreams?
8. What fantasies could bring excitement to your life?
9. List what you are passionate about experiencing.
10. List the people you enjoy being with.
11. What are the experiences or events you are looking forward to?

THREE: UNLEASH YOUR FEELINGS

1. How would you like to feel daily?
2. List the places that make you feel good.
3. What are the activities that bring you pleasure?
4. What are the experiences that bring you joy and happiness?

5.   Who are the people that inspire you?

6.   Who are the people that motivate you?

7.   What are the things, events or experiences that excite you?

8.   List the happiest moments in your life.

9.   What do you want to accomplish?

10. What opportunities do you see that will influence your life?

11. Who are the people that reinforce your ambitions and goals?

12. List the happiest people you have known in your life.

FOUR: DISCOVER YOUR PURPOSE

1.   List the principles that guide your decisions.

2.   Make a list of all the experiences or activities that interest you.

3.   List the talents that are important to you or that enrich your life.

4.   Make a list of your past accomplishments.

5.   List your personal strengths.

6.   What do you feel are your most important personal values?

7.   What are your most important beliefs?

8.   Which beliefs and values should be part of your philosophy?

9.   Which beliefs and values should be part of your creed?

10. What do you feel is your purpose in life?

11. Guided by your purpose, what is your mission in life?

12. What is most important to you?

13. Make a list of what or who brings meaning to your life.

14. List the questions that you need to answer.

FIVE: UNDERSTAND YOUR CURRENT REALITY

1.   List the problems that you are currently experiencing.

2.   Cross out the problems you can easily eliminate.

3.   What are you most worried about?

4.   List the obstacles that stand in your way.

5.   What do you find distracting that inhibits your success?

6.   What do you feel are your personal weaknesses?

7. What are you most afraid of?
8. What do you most regret having done or said?
9. What continues to give you guilt feelings?
10. What bad habits do you intend to eliminate?
11. What good habits do you intend to add to your life?
12. What routines need to be changed or modified?
13. Who are the people that are detrimental to your success?
14. What threats are you facing?
15. What routines or habits do you want to change or eliminate?
16. Who do you want to avoid?
17. List things about yourself you would like to change.
18. What would you like to change about your personal situation?
19. List things about the larger world you believe need to change.
20. List the important responsibilities that you need to reinforce.
21. What do you need to change to find your personal freedom?

SIX: UNLEASH YOUR CREATIVE SPIRIT

1. List areas where you want or need to be more creative.
2. List new activities that you want as part of your future.
3. List exciting new opportunities you want to take advantage of.
4. List things you would like to learn.
5. Where do you want to focus your curiosity?
6. What do you intend to accomplish in the next 12 months?
7. Which of your aspirations are the most significant?
8. List the people who will be part of your new future.
9. List the activities that will be part of your new future.
10. List the changes you intend to make.
11. List the questions you will need to answer.

SEVEN: UNLEASH YOUR NEW VISION

1. What exciting new visions do you have for your future?
2. What can you do to make your personal life more fulfilling?

3. What can you do to improve your health?
4. What can you do to support your family?
5. What are your professional development goals?
6. What can you do to advance in your career or business?
7. What are your new cultural and educational goals?
8. How can you enhance your spiritual life?
9. What are your financial objectives and goals?
10. What new things do you want to learn?

EIGHT: LIVE YOUR VISION

1. What activities are compatible with your vision?
2. Who brings joy to your life and reinforces your vision?
3. What are your most important priorities?
4. List the areas where your beliefs and actions are congruent.
5. What have you done to help other people or organizations?
6. What can you do to become more compassionate toward others?
7. List the areas in your life that are the most joyous and happy.
8. List the legacies you want to leave.
9. List the people who want to be in your plans for the future.
10. List your goals in priority order.
11. List experiences and goals that need to be in your Master Plan.

THE THREE CRUCIAL LISTS

After you have completed your self-evaluation, incorporated your dreams and desires into your future planning, and developed a vision for your future, conclude your research with these three crucial lists:

1. How do you want to feel? This is your most important list, reflecting and guiding your quality of life.

2. What do you want to accomplish? This provides direction for your life's purpose.

3. What actions are needed to achieve your intended accomplishments? These are the action plans that will help you reach your goals.

appendix c

READING LIST

Achor, Shawn. *Before Happiness*. New York: Random House, 2013.

—. *Big Potential*. New York: Penguin Random House, LLC, 2018.

Ben-Shahar, Tal. *Choose the Life You Want*. New York: The Experiment, LLC, 2012.

Birsel, Ayse. *Design the Life You Love*. Berkeley, CA: Ten Speed Press, 2015.

Buckingham, Will. *Happiness: A Practical Guide*. London: Icon Books Ltd., 2012.

Burnett, Bill, and Dave Evans. *Designing Your Life*. New York: Penguin Random House, LLC, 2016.

Chernoff, Marc, and Angel. *Getting Back to Happy*. New York: Penguin Random House, LLC, 2018.

Christensen, Clayton, James Allworth, and Karen Dillon. *How Will You Measure Your Life?* New York: HarperCollins, 2012.

Clear, James. *Atomic Habits*. New York: Penguin Random House, 2018.

Dolan, Paul, Ph.D. *Happiness by Design*. New York: Hudson Street Press, 2014.

Donnelly, Darrin. *Relentless Optimism*. Lenexa, KS: Shamrock New Media, Inc., 2017.

Dyer, Wayne W. *Excuses Begone! How to Change Lifelong, Self-Defeating Thinking Habits*. New York: Hay House, Inc., 2009.

—. *There's A Spiritual Solution to Every Problem*. New York: Harper-Collins, 2001.

—. *Wisdom of the Ages*. New York: HarperCollins Publishers, 1998.

Fletcher, Emily. *Stress Less, Accomplish More*. New York: HarperCollins Publishers, 2019.

Frankl, Viktor E. *Man's Search for Meaning*. Boston: Beacon Press, 2014 (originally published in 1958).

Freedman, Marc. *The Big Shift*. New York: Public Affairs, 2011.

Gilbert, Elizabeth. *Big Magic*. New York: Riverhead Books, 2015.

Hanh, Thich Nhat. *At Home in the World*. Berkeley, CA: Parallax Press, 2016.

—. *The Art of Living*. New York: HarperCollins Publishers, 2017.

Hardy, Darren. *The Compound Effect*. New York: Vanguard Press, 2010.

—. *The Entrepreneur Roller Coaster*. Lake Dallas, TX: Success, 2015.

Hicks, Esther, and Jerry Hicks. *Ask and It Is Given: Learning to Manifest Your Desires*. New York: Hay House, Inc., 2004

—. *The Law of Attraction: The Basics of the Teachings of Abraham*. New York: Hay House, Inc., 2006.

Kaufman, Scott Barry. *Wired to Create*. New York: Penguin Random House, LLC, 2015.

Kegan, Robert, and Lisa Laskow Lahey. *Unlocking Your Immunity to Change*. Boston: Harvard Business School Publishing Corporation, 2009.

Keller, Gary, with Jay Papason. *The One Thing*. Austin, TX: Bard Press, 2012.

Kerpen, Dave. *The Art of People.* New York: Crown Publishing Group, 2016.

Koch, Richard. *The 80/20 Principle.* New York: Random House, Inc., 1998.

—. *Living the 80/20 Way.* London: Nicholas Brealey Publishing, 2004.

LaPorte, Danielle. *The Fire Starter Sessions.* New York: Harmony Books, 2012.

—. *The Desire Map.* Boulder, CO: Sounds True, Inc., 2014.

Moore, Thomas. *A Religion of One's Own.* New York: Gotham Books, 2014.

—. *Ageless Soul.* New York: St. Martin's Press, 2017.

—. *Care of the Soul.* New York: HarperCollins Publishers, 1992.

Muller, Wayne. *How, Then, Shall We Live?* New York: Bantam Books, 1996.

Nelson, John E., and Richard N. Bolles. *What Color is Your Parachute?* New York: Ten Speed Press, 2010.

—. *What Color is Your Parachute? For Retirement.* Berkeley, CA: Ten Speed Press, 2007.

Proctor, Bob, with Sandra Gallagher. *The Art of Living.* New York: TarcherPerigee, LLC, 2015.

Ruffenach, Glenn, and Kelly Greene. *The Wall Street Journal Complete Retirement Guidebook.* New York: Three Rivers Press, 2007.

Ryan, M. J. *The Happiness Makeover.* Broadway Books, New York: MJF Books, 2005.

Seligman, Martin E. P. *Flourish.* New York: Simon & Schuster, Inc., 2011.

—. *The Hope Circuit.* New York: Public Affairs, 2018.

Sher, Barbara, with Barbara Smith. *I Could Do Anything If I Only Knew What It Was*. New York: Delacorte Press, 1994.

Shetty. Jay. *Think Like a Monk*. New York, Simon & Shuster, 2020.

Sinek, Simon. *Find Your Why*. New York: Portfolio/Penguin, 2017.

—. *The Infinite Game*. New York: Penguin Random House, 2019.

Swaback, Vernon D. *Believing in Beauty*. Phoenix, AZ: Bridgewood Press, 2009.

Tracy, Brian. *Focal Point*. New York: AMACOM, 2002.

—. *No Excuses*. Philadelphia: Da Capo Press, 2014.

Zadra, Dan, and Kobi Yamada. *One: How Many People Does It Take to Make a Difference?* Seattle, WA: Compendium, Inc., 2009.

Zalack, Richard. *Are You Doing Business or Building One?* Cleveland: Praxis, 2000.

Zelinski, Ernie J. *The Joy of Not Working*. Berkeley, CA: Ten Speed Press, 2003.

ACKNOWLEDGMENTS

This book is a story about my life, my philosophy, and many of my experiences as a designer, professor, and business executive. It has been a special privilege to have lived a life surrounded by visual excellence and beauty and to have worked in a profession that has reinforced my principles. Being part of a university environment has stimulated my curiosity and constantly involved me in the creative experience. I have been influenced by thousands of students and colleagues at the University of Illinois and the University of Akron who have reinforced my dedication to excellence in design and my respect for culture and the fine arts. In the business environment, I have worked with wonderful clients and exceptional writers, designers and marketing strategists who have contributed to my success and to the success of Kleidon & Associates.

The most important decision in my life was to join hands with my wife, Rose. We met while pursuing our undergraduate degrees at Illinois Wesleyan University. She has encouraged me, inspired me, and kept me moving forward in all my creative endeavors. Rose is a professor emeritus, writer, author, business executive, and the editor of this book, *Unleash Your Imagination.* Rose volunteered to edit my book, and I knew that with her experience as a writer, her knowledge of the subject, and her understanding of the author, she would be the perfect person to do so. And she was. I have been very fortunate to have Rose as my wife, editor, and life partner. I am grateful for all the insights and ideas she brought to the final version of this book. Her ability to see opportunities within the text, craft every sentence for clarity and make sure that each word was appropriate improved the book immensely. To have shared my life with such a wonderful person has indeed enhanced the quality of my life. We have been able to share our intellectual curiosity together. I am truly privileged.

Throughout my research for this book, I have been inspired by many people, and I want to offer my thanks for their influence and their dedication to their professions.

Shawn Achor	Darren Hardy	Martin Seligman
Bill Burnett	Robert Kegan	Simon Sinek
Darrin Donnelly	Lisa Laskow Lahey	Vernon Swaback
Wayne Dyer	Danielle LaPorte	Brian Tracy
Dave Evans	Thomas Moore	Mike Vance
Buckminster Fuller	Wayne Muller	Frank Lloyd Wright
Thich Nhat Hanh	Jim Rohn	Richard Zalack

Their books, audio tapes and presentations have been an inspiration. Coming from varied backgrounds and professions, they share a search for knowledge and a dedication to enhancing the quality of life. I encourage my readers to find their books in Appendix C, the Reading List.

And finally, I want to thank you, my readers, for investing your time to read this book. I hope that you have found ideas within the text that you will implement to enrich your lives. That has been my mission in writing this book – helping others to think creatively, unleash their imaginations and create lives guided by their deepest desires.

Made in United States
North Haven, CT
19 May 2022

19323611R00157